SPIRITUALITY FOR THE CLASSROOM:
From Research to Faith Development

SPIRITUALITY FOR THE CLASSROOM:
From Research to Faith Development

M. Wyn Moriarty, PhD

Modotti Press

Published by Modotti Press -- an imprint of Connor Court Publishing Pty Ltd

Copyright © M. Wyn Moriarty 2014

ALL RIGHTS RESERVED. This book contains material protected under International and Federal Copyright Laws and Treaties. Any unauthorised reprint or use of this material is prohibited. No part of this book may be reproduced or transmitted in any form or by any means, electronic or mechanical, including photocopying, recording, or by any information storage and retrieval system without express written permission from the publisher.

PO Box 224W
Ballarat VIC 3350
sales@connorcourt.com
www.connorcourt.com

ISBN: 9781925138436(pbk.)

Cover design by Maria Giordano

The painting on the cover, 'Wondering', is by Alec Stevenson © and first appeared in *Inklings: Doubt, Faith and Everyday Life* (Ed. MacNicol, 2014) used with permission

Printed in Australia

CONTENTS

Preface vii

Introduction xi

Acknowledgements xiii

Part 1: Perspectives on Spirituality 1

1 What is Spirituality? 3
2 Scriptural Understandings of Spirituality 27

Part 2: Introducing the Research 45

3 Reaching beyond Themselves: Consciousness and Relationality (1) 57
4 Reaching within Themselves: Consciousness and Relationality (2) 93
5 Charting the Path: "Roadmap", Values and Aspirations 119
6 "Footprints": Identity 143

Part 3: Nurturing Spirituality 165

7 Nurturing Children's Spirituality and Faith 167
8 Maintaining a Balance 207

Preface

A time of transition

> A leading Anglican layman and academic (Dr Peter Sherlock) has called for faith-based religious education taught by volunteers to be replaced by a critical, comprehensive, assessable study of religions taught by professionals (*The Melbourne Anglican*, April 2014).

Religious education in Australia is in a stage of transition which needs a creative and reforming response. This is the context and the challenge of this book.

Society in Australia in the early 21st century has made a transition from a nation of the English speaking Anglo-Celtic, largely Christian society, which held to the certainties of modern-age beliefs in science and rationality, to a society which is multicultural, post religious, and has largely abandoned core values in favour of the multiple choices of post-modernism. Recently, the challenge of this transition has been played out in the public arena on the issue of religious education in public schools. Australia has always been a secular society, in not having a state religion, but the term "secular" has come to be understood as meaning that religion has no place in our society, especially in our public schools. Furthermore, in an increasingly educated community, there are expectations that amateurs (volunteers) should be replaced by trained professionals where religion is taught in our classrooms.

The first issue which this book seeks to address is the need for all religious education teachers, and other professionals working in children's ministry, to be thoroughly and professionally qualified. It is assumed that all those who teach religious education in state or faith-based schools will be competent in educational theory and practice, and related areas such as understanding child development. Effective religious education does not indoctrinate children, but builds on contemporary educational practice in encouraging students to think critically, to solve problems for themselves and to learn collaboratively. Christian religious educators should also have adequate knowledge of the Bible and of the beliefs of their own faith community, and of other non-Christian faiths. Biblical knowledge should include some understanding of historical-critical scholarship, such as how to interpret the Bible in terms of the culture of the times of writing, and of the relevant literary genre of the text being studied. Religious education teachers also have a duty to be good role models of the faith they are teaching by paying attention to their own faith development. The faith development of the teacher is an underlying concern in this book, especially in the theological chapter 2 on Scriptural understanding of spirituality.

Secondly, a good professional religious education teacher needs to understand the spirituality of contemporary children, in order to enhance their wellbeing and possible growth in faith.

> The real challenge is to create an ambience entailing principal and teacher knowledge, attitudes and skills, as well as a physical environment and formal and informal curricula that allow and facilitate spiritual nurture. It entails new forms of training and in-service, enhancing intercultural and interfaith awareness and heightened sensitivity to building the kind of environment wherein, alongside all the other goals of schooling, spiritual development can be endorsed and supported (Tacey 2010, p. 25).

Formal religion has largely been abandoned in Western society, especially by the young, but there is a renewed interest in spirituality. Young people see the church as hierarchical, dogmatic and external to their lived experience. However, David Tacey (2003), an Australian sociologist, has noticed the rise in commitment to spirituality among the young. This spirituality is inclusive, spontaneous and not confined by religious institutions. It is personal, but not private, in that its adherents are concerned to be connected with the sacred, in nature and other people. However, its creativity and spontaneity needs to be provided with form. The challenge for the church is to provide grounding and a welcoming community for these young people. Religious education in schools is often the first forum in which children are introduced to the stories and beliefs of the Christian faith.

Children often exhibit this sense of wonder and connection with the natural world, other people, and an awareness of a spiritual world which may include a sense of the transcendent, or God. Their spontaneous and apparently innate sense of wonder, and connection with all things, needs to be observed and nurtured by people involved in teaching and children's ministry. The aim of this book is to promote this understanding.

Studying children's spirituality

In the last two decades there has been increased interest in spirituality, and children's spirituality in particular. A number of books have been written, from the point of view of research, or of practical concern about Christian education in schools, and nurture of children's faith in the home and in the church. This book seeks to build on the many excellent works which have emanated mainly from the United States, the United Kingdom, Canada and Australia. The focus of this book arises out of my recent research, which examined children's spirituality in the context of Australian children who attended state primary schools. These children were nearly all from non-religious family backgrounds so their spirituality was generally not expressed in religious terms, but drew on the Australian natural environment, secular Australian culture, and the multi-national mass media. This book examines the way the children in my research used these influences to fuel and express their innate spirituality. This book arises from the findings of my research, and long experience as a classroom teacher in secondary schools, mainly in the Catholic system, and as a volunteer Christian religious education teacher in state primary schools for more than ten years. In more recent times I have been associated with the research and practice in Children's Ministry through such organisations as the Port Philip West Children and Family Ministry network. Calling on these experiences, I seek to address some of the practical issues of nurturing the spirituality and faith development of children in the classroom. As I have had little experience in teaching multi-faith curricula I concentrate on delivering Christian religious education. However I have tried to keep adaptation to teaching about other faiths in mind.

This book addresses various understandings of what spirituality means, the findings of my recent research in children's spirituality, and some practical ways to nurture children's spirituality in the classroom.

References

Tacey, D. (2003). *The Spirituality Revolution: The Emergence of Contemporary Spirituality.* Sydney: HarperCollins.

Tacey, D. (2010). "Spirituality in a secular society", In M*eaning and connectedness: Australian perspectives on education and spirituality.* (Eds.) M. de Souza and J. Rimes. Mawson, ACT: Australian College of Education.

The Melbourne Anglican. "Anglican scholar urges end to volunteer-led RE". Melbourne, April 2014, No. 524.

Introduction

The aim of this book is to promote the enhancement of children's spirituality, firstly, by presenting an overview of recent scholarship in the fields of various social sciences, education, theology and children's ministry. There is an extensive summary of my own research to illustrate at first hand, the issues raised in the book. This is followed by a chapter outlining methods for promoting spiritual welfare and encouraging faith in the classroom. The book concludes with some observations by contemporary scholars of children's spirituality. While each section of the book is presented from the perspective of a particular academic discipline, the book as a whole aims to assist teachers of religious education, and other people in children's ministry, to engage in a spiritually motivated, and professionally skilled way, in order to minister to the children in their care.

Chapter One gives an overview of what is meant by spirituality from recent academic scholarship. This was the basis for my recent research into the spirituality of Victorian state primary school children. It provides a model for understanding of how to approach the religious education of contemporary children.

Chapter Two provides a Biblical perspective of the meaning of spirituality. This is to complement the often secular perspectives presented in the previous chapter with a focus on Christian faith. It is also written from a desire to strengthen the faith of workers in children's education and ministry, as they seek to communicate the good news of God's love to children.

Chapters Three to Six are included as a summary of my recent research. There is a brief introduction to the theory underlying my research. The following chapters provide extensive material taken from transcripts and analysis of interviews with children from Victorian state primary schools. It is hoped that this material will give teachers of religious education, and workers in children's ministry, a greater insight into the spirituality of contemporary children: their sense of wonder, the quality of their relationships, their values and aspirations, and the ways in which they find meaning in their lives. For some children this included religious faith.

Chapter Seven is designed to assist teachers in applying the content of the previous chapters to the ministry of nurturing the spirituality and faith of children in the classroom. This chapter calls on the experience of experts from a number of countries in the field of children's ministry, and includes some examples from my own experience as a teacher of Christian religious education. It deals with practical issues, such as classroom management, story-telling, and introduces various forms of prayer and times of silent reflection.

Chapter Eight presents material from two recent papers on children's spirituality which address some current issues, and complements the views expressed in the previous chapters concerning the enhancement of children's spirituality in the classroom. One concern is how to provide religious knowledge in a way that enhances, rather than inhibits children's personal religious experience. Another issue is how to address the shadow side of children's lives, such as external traumatic events or internal issues of failure and wrongdoing, in a way that is realistic but affirming of wellbeing and faith.

Reference

Moriarty, M.W. (2010). An investigation of the spirituality of children in Victorian state primary schools. PhD thesis, Australian Catholic University, Melbourne. dlibrary.acu.edu.au/digitalthesis/public/adt-acuvp291

Acknowledgements

I thank the publisher, Connor Court, for accepting this book, and especially Michael Gilchrist for his patience as editor. I wish to thank Dr Brendan Hyde, my research advisor, for his continued advice and encouragement in getting this book to publication. I also thank Dr Ian Weeks, Dr Charles Sherlock, Dr Vivienne Mountain, faculty members of the Australian Catholic University, and experts I have met through the International Association of Children's Spirituality, for help along the way. I acknowledge the assistance of the Centre for Theology and Ministry (CTM), Port Philip West Children's Ministry, and Chris Barnett in particular, for enabling me to keep in touch with advances in children's ministry. I am thankful for my years of experience in the classrooms at St Aloysius College, and through working for ACCESS Ministries in state primary schools, for what I have learned about religious education. Through my teaching experience, children and young people have brought me much wisdom and spiritual insight. I thank the principals, and staff at four Victorian schools for their cooperation in my research. And I especially thank the children who shared special moments of their lives with me. I thank the Anglican Parish of the Bellarine, and my many friends, for their encouragement over the years that this book has taken to come to fruition. Lastly, I thank my husband, Bill, and my daughter, Claire, for lovingly accompanying me on the journey.

PART 1

PERSPECTIVES ON SPIRITUALITY

1

WHAT IS SPIRITUALITY?

Introduction

As Christian religious educators, the primary sources for our understanding of spirituality are the Scriptures, and our own religious or spiritual experience. This will be explored in later chapters. Nevertheless, in the contemporary world it is helpful to explore the understanding of spirituality from other perspectives as well. This overview explores the understanding and experience of spirituality in Christianity in other ages, in other religions, and of people of no organised religion, and through the scientific study of spirituality through a number of contemporary academic disciplines. This will be followed in the next chapter by an exploration of our understanding of what the scriptures tell us about spirituality. This will be followed by a review of my research in contemporary children's spirituality.

This broader understanding of spirituality is helpful if we want to understand what spirituality means in the lives of children today and how teachers can tap into the reservoir of innate spirituality that modern researchers believe exists in all children. This understanding implies that the children in our classrooms are not "blank pages", but already have some awareness of God, or what we refer to as the

Transcendent[1], even if that awareness is sometimes blocked by the influence of a world which is largely indifferent or hostile toward God.

Prior to the commencement of my research project my own understanding of what is meant by the term "spirituality" was almost entirely formed by a conservative Christian tradition. However the current study of spirituality is much broader than that. Firstly, much of the current research in children's spirituality was conducted among children who were not growing up in this tradition. For example, Coles (1990) conducted interviews with 500 children from various national, religious and cultural backgrounds in America, Africa, Europe and the Middle East. Hay and Nye (2006) conducted research in England with children whose religious affiliation included Church of England, Muslim, Roman Catholic and no affiliation (2006, p. 87). Erricker, Erricker, Sullivan, Ota & Fletcher (1997) investigated the worldview, or spirituality of children in the United Kingdom in "rural schools and inner city schools, church schools and state schools, schools with a wide multicultural and multi-faith mix, and schools which lack such a perspective" (1997, p.21). Hyde (2008) conducted research in children's spirituality in Australia with children from a number of ethnic and religious traditions who were attending Catholic schools. Secondly, under the influences of secularisation and multiculturalism, spiritual expression in Western societies is becoming more diverse, more personal, and less likely to be affiliated with organised religion (Tacey, 2003). Thirdly, the academic study of spirituality is no longer confined to theologians, but has extended to other disciplines, such as Psychology and Neurophysiology.

This chapter explores some of the perspectives of what is meant by spirituality. The emphasis is largely on Christian spirituality, since

---

[1] The *Macquarie Dictionary* defines "transcendent" as "being beyond matter, and having a continuing existence therefore outside the created world". The term can refer to God, heavenly beings, etc.

this is my own perspective, and the purpose of this book is to enhance the teaching of Christian religious education. However, perspectives other than Christian are also discussed. This chapter explores the meaning of spirituality under the following headings

- Spirituality as human longing for something more.
- Understanding spirituality from various academic perspectives.
- Spirituality as relationship in modern perspectives.
- Everyday spirituality: being a child.

Spirituality as human longing for something more

Spirituality in Christian tradition

Traditionally, spirituality has been seen as an aspect of religion. Search for union with the transcendent or infinite is common to all religions.

From an early Christian perspective, St Augustine (354-430 CE) expressed this longing for something more in his *Confessions*.

> Who, O Lord, will grant that I may repose in thee? Who will grant that thou mayest enter into my heart and inebriate it, that I may forget all my wicked ways and embrace thee, my only good? (Augustine, 1965, Book 1, p. 34).

This extract illustrates the two-way relationship between God and human beings that is central to Christian spirituality. As the human being searches to be united to God, God enters and unites with the human spirit. In this extract from Augustine one finds other key features of Christian spiritually. Spirituality can be experienced as repose, or stillness, and also as heightened emotion. Christians believe that this communion with God is possible through God's initiative and God's grace, for God forgives and heals our "wicked ways" (see quote above) which are a barrier to our communion with God.

While Christians' "longing for more" is a longing to experience God in some "heavenly realm" it is also a longing to experience God in daily life, an involvement of the whole person. Rowan Williams (1979), a former Archbishop of Canterbury, stated that Christian spirituality is not

> an escape into the transcendent, a flight out of history and the flesh, but the heart of its meaning is a human story... an odd and ambivalent story, which becomes open to interpretation in terms of God's saving work (1979, p. 2).

The goal of Christian life becomes not only enlightenment but wholeness, a wholeness of life in this world, lived as consequence of a past historical event and in hope of a future fulfilment of the saving relationship with Jesus Christ that has begun (Williams, 1979). Therefore for Williams, Christian spirituality is "about the whole of life: it must touch every area of human experience, public and social, the painful, negative, even pathological byways of the mind, the moral and relational world" (1979, p. 2).

Mysticism

For some people, spirituality is a mystical experience: that is, an extraordinary moment of sensing the presence of God or a higher power. This experience may be a vision, or voices or something like a sense of being out of body, space and time, being in union with the transcendent. Through the ages people from many faith traditions have had mystical experiences. For Christian mystics this longing for something more has been fulfilled in reaching great moments of experience of union or communion with God.

One such mystic was Julian of Norwich, an anchoress or recluse, who lived in England from approximately 1342 to after 1413 (Julian, 1966). In 1373 she experienced a severe illness, and at that time she received sixteen revelations or "shewings". These became the basis for her spiritual reflection and writing. In most of these revelations

Julian had graphic visions of the sufferings of Christ, and insights into the meaning of the love of Christ as revealed in his Passion. Her visions came upon her unexpectedly. Her visions were visually very vivid and emotional in content, and she had a strong sense of their meaning, and divine source. They also filled her with joy and renewed her faith. Julian exhibited characteristics of a mystic in openness and longing for union with the transcendent, and the willingness to share with others the wisdom she acquired through mystical experiences.

Other famous Christian mystics include Ignatius Loyola, Teresa of Avila and St John of the Cross. These saints are known to us, not only through their visions and special revelations. They are known to us through their lives of practical holiness in the everyday world, together with their writings about their disciplined devotion to prayer as an example for others to follow, even in the contemporary world.

Evelyn Underhill (1949), a 20th century pioneer in the scientific study of mysticism, described such experience as follows:

> It began by the awakening within the self of a new and embryonic consciousness: a consciousness of divine reality … She (the self) opened her eyes upon a world still natural, but no longer illusory; since it was perceived to be illuminated by the Uncreated Light. She knew then the beauty, the majesty, the divinity of the living World of Becoming which holds in its meshes every living thing (Underhill, 1949, pp. 448, 449).

The experience of mystics has some relevance to children's spirituality. The relevance is not in the years of arduous spiritual exercises undertaken by the great mystics, but rather in the possibilities which arise from children's openness to wonder and new ways of seeing the transcendent as it appears for them in the ordinary events of life.

Spirituality as universal

This longing for something more is not restricted to Christians, but scholars have discovered that it is a universal phenomenon. The 20th century Catholic monk, Bede Griffiths (1994), outlines the universal nature of spirituality in the main world religions.

> This reality (which) has no proper name, since it transcends the mind and cannot be expressed in words, was called Brahman and Atman (the Spirit) in Hinduism, Nirvana and Sunyata (the Void) in Buddhism, Tao (the Way) in China, Being (toōn) in Greece and Yahweh ("I am") in Israel, but all these are but words which point to an inexpressible mystery … the goal of all human striving, the truth which all science and philosophy seeks to fathom, the bliss in which all human love is fulfilled (Griffiths, 1994, p. 8).

Over the centuries each of the world religions has developed in different physical and cultural environments, and extended these spiritual insights to produce their great doctrinal systems and religious practices. But Griffiths maintained that there is a remarkable commonality of spiritual experience underlying the differences, which he called "perennial philosophy" (1994, p. 8). Griffiths summarised a universal pattern by which spirituality is expressed through the various world religions. This pattern includes first of all the "supreme Principle, the ultimate truth, beyond name and form" variously called the Nirguna Brahman in Hinduism, the Nirvana in Buddhism, The Reality – al Haqq – of Sufi Islam, the Godhead of Christianity. Secondly, there is the manifestation of the hidden Reality, the Saguna Brahman of Hinduism, the Buddha of Buddhism, the Sikh Guru, the personal God, Yahweh or Allah, of Judaism and Islam, and the Christ of Christianity. Thirdly there is the Spirit, the *atman* of Hinduism, the "compassion" of the Buddha, the "Breath of the Merciful" in Islam, and the Holy Spirit in Christianity. Finally in each religion this universal truth is embodied, not just in individual believers, but in a community, where spirituality finds expression through the structures of ritual and doctrine (1994, p. 42). Progress has been made, since the middle of the 20th century, towards understanding the common spiritual features of all religions.

In everyday life, most Christians are more aware of the differences between religions than what they have in common. We generally believe that the Christian faith is unique in that we believe that "there is no other name under heaven given among mortals by which we must be saved" (Acts 4:12). This is generally interpreted as meaning that the way to God and salvation is provided only by Jesus Christ, and his death and resurrection. However, in the same book of Acts there are also hints that people of other faiths can be led by the Holy Spirit toward knowledge of God. For example, in Paul's sermon at Athens, he reminds his hearers that God gives life, and a desire to know him to people in all times and places "so that they would search for God and perhaps grope for him and find him – though he is not far from each one of us" (Acts 17: 27).

An understanding of spirituality as operating in other religions, and in people of no organised religion, helps the religious education teacher to look for bridges between Christianity and other faiths in the classroom setting. It is helpful to assume that there is a spark of spirituality in all of the children in the class, rather than looking on them as a blank page on which we have to write the elements of the faith. In our own culture this spark may be a sense of wonder at the marvels of the natural world or of scientific discovery. While children of western, nominally Christian background may be reluctant to discuss religion, children from other faith cultures are usually happy to discuss their understanding of God or of worship. For example, where an Australian will start a conversation with a stranger by discussing the weather or sport, an Indian person will probably ask "Who do you worship?" In the classroom a comparison of the religious customs or spiritual understanding of different children can be a bridge to discussing these things in a Bible story.

Summary

"Longing for something more" has been the experience of many people throughout history. In the Christian tradition Augustine of Hippo and Julian of Norwich are two of many people expressed this longing through daily life and through heightened mystical experiences. Mystical experiences occur both spontaneously and in response to a life of disciplined prayer. A longing for unity with ultimate, or integral, reality is found in all religious traditions, so that scholars such as Griffiths describe this characteristic of spirituality as universal.

Understanding spirituality from various academic perspectives

The universal nature of spirituality has been studied by scholars of various disciplines, demonstrating the many ways the human "longing for something more" can be understood. Many scholars have attempted to discover the origins of spirituality in pre-history and human development. The anthropologist, Mircea Eliade's studies of tribal people uncovered patterns of ritual and myth which expressed an underlying understanding of a cosmic power as manifesting itself alike in nature and in man, and which is responsible for the fertility of the earth, the changes of the seasons. This power is also the source of moral law and tribal ritual. According to Eliade, this awareness of the sacred is not just a product of the rational, conscious mind, but the experience of the whole person (Cited in Griffiths 1994, p. 12).

The philosopher, Rudolph Otto, identified the overwhelming feeling, such as Abraham had when confronted with God, when he said "I am but dust and ashes" (Genesis 18:27), as "creature consciousness" (Otto, 1923/1958, p. 10). This sense of creaturehood leads to a sense of a transcendent Other, for which Otto coined the term "numinous". The presence of the numinous is experienced as awe and fear ("mysterium tremendum"), but also as joy and fascination.

This longing to experience this "something more" appears to be a universal spiritual phenomenon.

> This insight shows that above and beyond our rational being lies hidden the ultimate and highest part of our nature, which can find no satisfaction in the mere allaying of the needs of our sensuous, psychical, or intellectual impulses and cravings. The mystics called it the basis or ground of the soul (Otto, 1958, p. 36).

A brief summary will show that scientists and thinkers from many fields have contributed something to our understanding of spirituality as a human characteristic. The Catholic theologian, Bernard Lonergan, presented an intellectual understanding of spirituality as the highest form of reason. Carl Jung, the famous psychoanalyst described the Self as the regulator of the human spirit. The investigations of Alister Hardy, a biologist, suggested that the occurrence of spirituality is the natural result of evolutionary adaptation. Helminiak, a psychologist and theologian, clarified some differences between human spirituality and the divine being as spirit. The neurologists, Zohar & Marshall, and Newberg and his associates, documented evidence that observable brain functions occur during spiritual experiences, leading Zohar & Marshall to conclude that the brain is the physiological seat of human spirituality. Ken Wilber (2001) concluded that all scientific disciplines lead to a model of human spirituality where the Self has the ultimate unifying role. Most of these scholars conclude that spirituality can be studied through the various scientific disciplines, and that human spirituality has an adaptive function of uniting the different human faculties, for the wellbeing of the individual and the species.

Spirituality as relationship, modern perspectives

During the 20th century understanding of spirituality saw an emphasis on its relational aspects: relationship with the transcendent and within the Divine Trinity, relationship with other people and with the earth. There has also been a shift from understanding spirituality only in a religious context to recognising spiritual experiences as common to all humanity. Early research into the nature of relationship with the transcendent can be traced to William James, whose famous lectures entitled *Varieties of Religious Experience* were published in 1902. James was one of the first scholars to carry out psychological studies of religious experiences, that is, the study of relationships of people with God. James' aim was to defend the reality of subjective spiritual experience against the prevailing thinking of his time, which claimed that the only reality was what could be proved by logic or scientific observation. James showed, from many first-hand examples, that there is variety of religious experiences of relationship with the divine, such as conversion, or mystical encounter, which cannot be accounted for by logic alone. James attempted to capture people's spiritual experiences by recording their variety, and allowing each individual the freedom to express his or her own experiences in their own way. James understood relationship with the God to be the result of a spontaneous encounter with the transcendent Other. James discovered some common features of mystical experience, which he described as follows:

- Ineffable – a state which words cannot adequately describe.
- Neotic – a (new) state of knowledge, insight or certainty. This change is marked by moral growth.
- Transient – a state which cannot be sustained for long, and cannot always be recalled clearly. Its passing may result in a temporary reaction of depression.
- Passive – a state which the mystic feels is "given", and is not the result of his or her willing it. He or she is overwhelmed by what Wordsworth called "a power that disturbed" (James, 1928, pp. 380,381; Priestley, 2001, pp. 189-191).

James' insights into the variety and spontaneous nature of spirituality have relevance when examining contemporary spiritual experiences, such as those of the children in recent studies. James conducted his studies in the predominantly Protestant society of the United States at the beginning of the 20th century, a society which assumed that a religious experience meant a Christian experience of God. However, the experiences he described were not dissimilar to the variety of experiences of an "unseen reality" experienced by people today. The children in my study did not come from religious Christian families. Some came from families of other faith traditions, but most appeared to come from families of no religious allegiance. However, most of the children demonstrated a sense of awe and wonder, of joy, and of "the reality of the unseen" that James spoke about. The children expressed their experiences of such a reality through their life stories and through the stories and symbols of the culture in which they live. Many of these stories came from books they had read, or television, film or videogames that they had experienced. The children used stories from these sources to explain their sense of meaning or higher reality.

The 20th century saw a change of emphasis from focusing only on the relationship with the transcendent to spirituality which also encompassed relationship with other people and with the natural world. Thomas Merton provided an example of a 20th century contemplative monk whose spiritual journey was marked by tension between his longing for solitude to enrich his relationship with God, and his other vocation as a writer, which brought him into ever closer relationship with the world outside the monastery (Del Prete, 1990). In Merton's writings there is a theme of unity: unity with nature, with the suffering world, and with other faiths, and his own journey towards unity with God. Merton played an active role in the wider community in confronting Americans with the moral choices of his time, such as those presented by the Vietnam War and the threat of nuclear war. Merton saw his spirituality in being united with other people as follows. "I must look for my identity, somehow, not only in God, but in other men [sic]. I will never be able to find myself if I isolate myself from the rest of mankind" (*New Seeds of Contemplation*, in Forrest, 1991, p. 118). He was also aware of the unity of the created world with God and with himself. He wrote: "A tree gives glory to God first of all by being a tree. For in being what God means it to be, it is obeying Him. It 'consents', so to speak, to His creative love" (*New Seeds of Compassion*, in Forrest, 1991, p. 109).

Merton's spirituality included dialogue between his Catholic faith and Eastern religions, particularly Zen Buddhism. He found certain features of Christian mystical experience to be similar to transcendent experiences in Buddhism. Merton explains that "in the Christian experience the focus of this 'experience' is found not in the individual self as a separate, limited and temporal ego, but in Christ, or the Holy Spirit, 'within' this self. True life is the freedom that transcends the self and resides in *"the other"* by love (Merton, 1961, p. 9). "To find the full meaning of our existence we must find not the meaning we expect but the meaning that is revealed to us by God; the meaning that comes to us out of the transcendent darkness of His mystery and our own" (1961, p. 6). In his life and his writings Merton exemplified the paradox that in "losing one's self" a person finds his true self, and spiritual relationship with God and others.

A collection of stories of some 20th century woman mystics (Bancroft, 1989) revealed the great variety of ways in which spirituality is expressed in our time. In common with mystics in all times and places, these women had a longing for unity with the Transcendent. This ultimate Unity was described in various ways. Toni Packer, who was influenced by Zen Buddhism, described it as "in-touchness with what's there", or a state of no self. Evelyn Underhill, who was influenced by ancient philosophers like Plato and Plotinus, and by Christianity, preferred the term "unity with Reality". These women identified the object of their unity in a variety of ways. Meinred Craighead, who had American Indian ancestry, maintained a Christian identity but always referred to God as the Mother, or the Great Spirit. The Mother was a protector from the patriarchal values of Christianity, whom she related to through female and earth symbols such as blood, water, earth and its vegetation and animals, and the cycles of the moon. For Simone Weil, the object of her contemplation was the suffering Christ. Her own bodily suffering, and entering into the suffering of others, enabled her to enter into "the unimaginable beauty" of Gregorian chants so that "in the course of these services the thought of the Passion of Christ entered into my being once and for all" (1989).

Spirituality provided a path of personal liberation for each of these women, and they shared what they had learned with others. Raine was able to express and share her spiritual experiences of seeing the beauty of the natural world through her poetry, as Craighead did through art and poetry. Weil and Underhill related to others through their writing, and others by instructing enquirers who came to them. These women did not isolate themselves, but spread their love and concern for the suffering and need of other people and the planet. These features of connectedness and compassion, are not exclusively feminine virtues, but are features of mystical unity with all things: the Divine and the created

Contemporary spirituality outside the mainstream religions

A characteristic of much contemporary spiritual experience is that it is recognised in people who are not affiliated with organised religion. Tacey's (2003) observation of Australian young people found that at the same time as they are abandoning formal religion, they are increasingly embracing spirituality. For these young people spirituality means "our relationship with the sacredness of life, nature, and the universe, and this relationship is no longer confined to formal devotional practice or to institutional places of worship…(spirituality) is an inclusive term, covering all pathways that lead to meaning and purpose" (2003, p. 38). This spirituality allows the sacred to enter their lives and experiences. This sacredness can include "ecology, nature and the physical world, or the stars, plants and stellar cosmology, or the search for the inner or true self, or the quest for mystical experiences" (2003, p. 80). Youth spirituality, as Tacey described it, is personal, but not private, but an engaged spirituality, concerned with the welfare of the world and the sacredness of endangered life, and social issues like racism and wars (2003, p. 66). For Tacey, the positive features of this kind of spirituality is that it is essentially incarnational[2], in its deep and personal engagement with the sacredness of self and the created world, which strives for wholeness and integration (2003, p. 79).

However, Tacey believed that this contemporary spirituality is one-sided, being susceptible to the excesses and trivialising of much New Age spirituality, and lacks the roots and guidance that organised religion can provide. It also lacks a realistic sense of evil as well as of good (2003, p. 85). Tacey (1995) lamented that "society becomes a demonic parody of sacred reality when society no longer recognises the divine sources from which its own life springs" (1995, p. 177). Therefore the new interest in spirituality exhibited by the young needs to be directed towards "connection to our life-sustaining roots" (2003, p. 226), to faith in God through traditional religion, that is, life within the church, for the wellbeing of individuals, society and the earth.

The present concerns about climate change and the degradation of the environment have led to a renewed interest in spirituality which involves our relationship with the earth, and all living things. However,

---

[2] "Incarnation" for Christians usually refers to the coming of Jesus Christ as God become a human being, from the Latin word for flesh. A Macquarrie dictionary definition of "incarnation" is "assumption of human form or nature, as for a divine being". It is sometimes extended to mean the presence of God in other physical life-forms.

there have always been traditional nature spiritualities which have a sense of connection to the earth. Indigenous people, such as the Australian aborigines, have always had a relationship with the spirit of the earth. Patrick Dodson, an aboriginal leader, said:

> The land is a living place made up of sky, clouds, rivers, trees, the wind, the sand; and the Spirit has planted my own spirit there, in my own country. It is something – and yet it is not a thing – it is a living entity. It belongs to me. I belong to it (Dodson, 1973, quoted by *The Rainbow Spirit Elders*, 2007, p. 32).

Concern for the environment is not only an issue of personal connection with the land, but for some people is also about relationship with God as creator, which has ethical and political implications about the community's management of the earth and its resources. John Avard is a Victorian farmer who wrote:

> I see in nature – a wonderful, powerful, patient, Creator God. It's a process of continual conversion from self to other. Christians are often very un-Christian on the farm. We can still see raping and pillaging of the land. There's a lack of wisdom, or there is intentional blindness in government handling of environmental issues (Avard, quoted in *Earthsong Journal* 2007).

In the foreword to Conlon's *Earth story: Sacred story* (1994), Thomas Berry observed that in the late 20th century people were suffering a dislocation from a sense of the sacred, and need to return to an understanding of the mystery and meaning of the universe as having a primordial consciousness as well as a physical dimension. For

> the universe as a whole is implicated in every manifestation and every activity of the universe ... (human beings) have an immediate presence to every being in the universe individually and to the universe itself in its unity. Every atom

is immediately present to every atom in the universe (Berry, cited in Conlon, 1994, p. vii).

Conlon (1994) elaborated three patterns of this interconnectedness with the universe. *Differentiation* means that every rock, snowflake or person is different, and therefore to be valued as a unique manifestation of the divine. *Interiority* means that each created subject has a capacity for deep interior experience – to recognise and listen to our own inner voice, and to each member of the Earth community. *Community* means we are bonded together in relationship with other human beings, the natural world, and all that is (1994, pp. 18, 19). In Christian tradition the Trinity is understood as a dynamic oneness of God, expressed as a community of equality and diversity. Conlon understood that there is a direct connection between the dynamic patterns of the universe (differentiation, interiority and communion) and the Trinity (1994, p.20).

Summary

This section discussed spirituality as relationship with the sacred Other through mystical encounters or everyday experiences, within or outside religious tradition. This sacred Other may mean God, the earth and its creatures, or other human beings. Relationship with the transcendent in its many forms was explored by James. Living out a mystical relationship was exemplified by Merton, and various modern female mystics. Characteristics of these lives included relating to the ordinary world in an ethical way in the light of transcendental experiences, and finding the inspiration for these experiences in many places: in Christianity, in other religions and outside of religious tradition. Particular characteristics of modern spirituality include an emphasis on finding an individual meaning for living, and a return to the sources of transcendental relationship in the natural world.

Everyday spirituality: being a child

A definition of spirituality

This chapter began with Rowan Williams' statement that Christian spirituality is not "an escape into the transcendent, a flight out of history and the flesh, but the heart of its meaning is a human story" (Williams, 1979, p. 2). The human story, as an indicator of spirituality in the life of the children in various recent studies, was the story of their day-to-day lives. This meant their relationships with their families and their peers, and the struggle of everyday Being-in-the-world.

Brendan Hyde, a contemporary Australian Catholic scholar (2008) summarised his understanding of the spirituality of children as follows:

> My understanding is that children's spirituality is an ontological reality and involves a path towards the realisation of the true Self, in which ultimately, Self is unified with everything that is Other than Self (Hyde, 2008, p. 44).

This quote highlights two aspects of spirituality: *self-realisation* and *relationship* or communion with others. The German philosopher, Martin Heidegger (1980) sheds some light on the aspect of self-realisation, the reality of spirituality as being human, when he explored the mystery of Being. He used the term "Dasein" to describe the human phenomenon of self-understanding, or what might be described as reflecting on what it means to be Me. This self-understanding takes place "within a world", a particular time (temporality) and place, which Heidegger calls "everydayness" (1980, p. 38). This process of self-understanding, of relating to oneself as a continuing identity, as "I", is seen in the findings of my research as a key feature of spirituality.

On the other hand, Webster (2005), based on the writings of Heidegger and others, argued that a spiritual understanding is more than self regard; it is relational. Personal identity is not just "What am

I?" that is, "I am a woman" or "I am a teacher". It is best understood as "Who am I?" which is relational in character: to whom am I important? I know myself to be "Wyn" because that was what my parents, and later my friends, called me. I know myself to be a sister to X, a wife to Y, and a friend to Z. It is in the way these significant people talk to me and relate to me that I have an understanding of what sort of person I am. I also know myself as a scholar because I am writing this book, and a Christian through my relationship with Jesus Christ and other Christians. Webster stated that "personal identity should be understood to be embedded in the purposes one has for one's life through *how* one relates, and is therefore spiritual" (2005, p. 5). Evidence of this spiritual capacity for both self-regard and a sense of identity through relationship with others were found among the children in my research. Hyde (2008) expressed this phenomenon as "a path towards the realisation of the true Self, in which ultimately, Self is unified with everything that is Other than Self" (Hyde, 2008, p. 44).

Some theologies of childhood

In an age where spirituality is commonly acknowledged, but largely divorced from religious traditions, there is a twofold desire: within educational circles to nurture the spirituality of children and young people, and within religious institutions to reconnect children and young people with their faith traditions (Yust, Johnson, Sasso & Roehlkepartain, 2006, p. 3). There is a renewed interest among scholars of children's spirituality, as well as within the various religious communities, to reflect on the meaning of spirituality within and between faith traditions (2006).

A brief review of the major religions (Yust et al. 2006) indicated that although most religious traditions do not have a well developed theology of childhood (or theory about the relationship of God to children), sacred texts call for the care and nurture of children, and members of each of the communities value the instruction and initiation of children into the faith community. From a Christian perspective, Marcia Bunge (2006) argued that "the church has not developed theologies of childhood that acknowledge the needs and vulnerabilities of children, as well as the gifts and strengths they bring to families and communities" (p. 53). Bunge presented six different and often conflicting Christian perspectives of childhood:

- Gifts of God and signs of God's blessing, and sources of blessing to their parents.
- Sinful creatures (who have therefore sometimes been abused), but also moral agents with growing responsibility for their actions.
- Developing beings who need instruction in the faith, and guidance in virtuous living.
- Fully human from infancy, therefore to be respected as made in the image of God.
- Models of faith and sources of revelation, whose wisdom can be a challenge to adults.
- Vulnerable human beings in need of protection, justice and compassion.

(Bunge, 2006, pp. 58-62).

These perspectives of childhood are shared by other religious traditions.[3] For example, in the various strands of Hinduism deities have manifested themselves as children or youths, and therefore children are models of faith and revelation. Children are seen as having latent spirituality through their "karma" inherited from

---

[3] These views were outlined by various authors within the various faith traditions in a book entitled *Nurturing child and adolescent spirituality: Perspectives from the world's religious traditions,* (2006) edited by Yust K., Johnson A., Sasso, S., & Roechlkepartain. N . Lanham, ML: Rowman & Littlefield.

previous lives. In Buddhist tradition children may enter the life of the religious communities of monks. Children are seen as "metaphors" for the lower stages of spiritual development, and also as Bodhisatvi, or sources of inspiration and enlightenment. Jewish children are seen as a source of blessing, and an inspiration as signs of God's relationship with the people of Israel. They also have ritual and moral obligations within the religious community, and need to be given instruction in the Law. In Islamic tradition children are valued because they were loved by the Prophet. Children are born innocent, and have the capacity to know God and lead a spiritual life. But they need adult guidance and example in the practice of the faith, and protection from evil influences, to reach their spiritual potential. This brief overview demonstrated that in the world religions children may not have a central place in theological reflection, but they are valued for their place in the sacred texts and as sources of blessing to the communities. Children are recognised as innately spiritual, but who need the community's guidance if they are to reach their full potential.

Jerome Berryman (2005) presented a fuller reflection on the lack of a Christian theology of childhood, and this tradition's ambiguity about the nature of childhood. He noted the "low view" that children are born with the taint of original sin but could become good through baptism and grace, as emphasised by Augustine. There is also the "high view" of childhood, as propagated by Rousseau, that children were born good and became evil under the influence of society (p. 118). Berryman explored the attitude of Jesus to children, as recorded in the Gospels, where Jesus welcomed children and blessed them (Mark 10: 13-16), and encouraged his followers to "become like a child" (Matthew 18:3), and to exercise humility, in order to enter the kingdom of heaven. Berryman maintained that, in the light of these and other biblical references to children, a contemporary view of the spirituality of children can be developed by "noticing children around us and remembering our own childhood" (p. 131). From his many years of teaching children by "Godly Play" Berryman presented three ways of understanding and encouraging children's spirituality, and extending this to understanding adult spirituality also. The first way is derived from the children's game of "peek-a-boo", which demonstrates the theological insight that "God is hidden yet also present" (p. 131). The second way is in the example of "the silent child", which demonstrates that for any relationship with children and adults, non verbal communication is as necessary as verbal communication, and there should be consistency between the two modes. (Our actions and gestures are just as important as our words). Thirdly, Berryman explored the importance of relationships which include "an ethic of blessing" which often includes physical contact, (such as placing a hand on the child's head), and provides a guide for our action and development on life's journey (p. 132). Thus, Berryman turned the usual model of spiritual education on its head, suggesting that not only can children learn from their relationships with adults, but adults can learn from children.

Elaine Champagne, a Canadian researcher, (2003, 2005) also presented theological reflection on the meaning of spirituality for young children. She challenged the commonly held idea that a person has to be self-aware to be spiritual. From her observations of very young children, aged 3 to 6, Champagne asserted that they are spiritually aware simply by *being alive*. This observation also applies to the older children in my study, who are only just becoming self aware. When Champagne maintained that young children are spiritual by virtue of *"being alive"*, she compared this awareness to Heidegger's (1980) ideas about *being-in-the-world*, their *Dasein*. Young children's spirituality is expressed unselfconsciously through three *modes of being: Sensitive, Relational* and *Existential*. The *Sensitive* mode means "expressing who they are through their bodies" (2003, p. 45), through their voices, their facial and bodily expressions, and through drawings and sculptures. The *Relational* mode of being is expressed in the special way young children relate to adults and other children, through showing affection, rejection, forgiving, having special affinity with particular people, and looking to significant adults to provide safety and meaning in their world. The *Existential* mode of being refers to young children's capacity to relate to time and space and to find meaning in life through games and imagination. Champagne believed that as the child lives in the present, he or she is fulfilling the spiritual purpose in life of *being-a-child*, which can be an opening into the ultimate "knowing" of being part of the Kingdom of God (2003, p. 52). Champagne concluded that "Reflecting on the meaning of their *being-a-child* can enrich us with renewed perspectives on our own *being-in-the-world*" (p. 52). This is an ultimate goal of the study of spirituality.

Summary

This section examined spirituality as a quality of being, in everyday life, for all people, but particularly for children. This began with Hyde's (2008) summary of spirituality as an "ontological" or essential reality, not just a special psychological state, that is, who one is, not how one feels. Heidegger refers to this state of being as mediated by Dasein or self-reflection. Yust and other writers (Yust et al. 2006) explored the understanding of children's spirituality from within the world's main religious traditions. From within the Christian tradition, Champagne (2003) and Berryman (2005) believed that children are already in a spiritual state of being, in the immediacy of the experience of being a child. Both of these writers stressed the Christian community's responsibility to nurture the spontaneous spirituality of children.

References

Augustine of Hippo. (1923/1965). *The Confessions of St Augustine.* (T. Matthew, Trans., R. Huddleston, Revised Trans.). London: Collins/Fontana.

Bancroft, A. (1989). *Weavers of Wisdom: Women Mystics of the Twentieth Century.* London: Penguin.

Berryman, J. (2005). *Godly Play: An Imaginative Approach to Religious Education.* Minneapolis, MI: Augsburg Press.

Bunge, M. (2006). The dignity and complexity of children: Constructing Christian theologies of childhood. In K. Yust, A. Johnson, S. Sasso, & E. Roehlkepartain (Eds.) *Nurturing Child and Adolescent Spirituality: Perspectives from the World's Religious Traditions.* (pp. 53-68). Lanhan, MD: Rowman & Littlefield.

Champagne, E. (2003). Being a child: A spiritual child. *International Journal of Children's Spirituality. 8* (1), 43-53.

Coles, R., (1990). *The Spiritual Life of Children.* London: Harper Collins.

Conlon, J. (1984). *Earth Story: Sacred Story.* Mystic, CT: Twenty-third Publications.

Del Prete, T. (2002). *Thomas Merton and the Education of the Whole Person.* Birmingham, AL: Religious Education Press.

Erricker, C., Erricker, J., Sullivan, D., Ota, K., Fletcher, M. (1997). *The Education of the Whole Child.* London: Cassell.

Forrest, J. (1991). *Living with Wisdom: A Life of Thomas Merton.* Maryknoll, NY: Orbis.

Griffiths, B. (1994). *Universal Wisdom: A Journey Through the Sacred Wisdom of the World.* London: Harper Collins.

Hay, D & Nye, R. (2006). *The Spirit of the Child,* (Rev. ed.) London: Jessica Kingsley.

Heidegger, M. *Being and Time.* (1980). (J. Macquarrie & E. Robinson Trans.) Oxford: Blackwell.

Hyde, B. (2008). *Children and Spirituality: Searching for Meaning and Connectedness*. London: Jessica Kingsley.

James, W. (1902/1928). *The Varieties of Religious Experience: A Study in Human Nature*. New York, NY: Longmans, Green and Co.

Julian of Norwich. (1966/1988). *Revelations of Divine Love*. (C. Wolters, Ed.). London: Penguin.

Merton, T. (1961). *The New Man*. New York: Farrer, Straus & Giroux.

Otto, R. (1923/1958). *The Idea of the Holy*. (J. Narvey Trans.). London: Oxford University Press.

Priestley, J. (2001). The experience of religious varieties: William James and the post-modern age. In J. Erricker, C. Ota, & C. Erricker (Eds.). *Spiritual Education: Culture, Religion and Social Differences: A New Perspective for the Twenty-First Century*. (pp. 184-194). Brighton, UK: Sussex Academic.

Robinson, E. (1977). *The Original Vision: A Study of the Religious Experience of Childhood*. Oxford: The Religious Experience Research Unit.

Tacey, D. (1995). *The Edge of the Sacred: Transformation in Australia*. Sydney: HarperCollins.

Tacey, D. (2003). *The Spirituality Revolution: The Emergence of Contemporary Spirituality*. Sydney: Harper Collins.

Underhill, E. (1911/1949). *Mysticism: A Study in the Nature and Development of Man's Spiritual Consciousness*. London: Methuen & Co.

Webster, R.S. (2005). Personal identity: moving beyond essence. *International Journal of Children's Spirituality. 10 (1)*, 5-16.

Wilber, K. (2001). *The Eye of Spirit: An Integral Vision of a World Gone Slightly Mad*. Boston: Shambala.

Williams, R. (1979). *The Wound of Knowledge: Christian Spirituality from the New Testament to St John of the Cross*. London: Darton, Longman & Todd.

Yust, K., Johnson, A., Sasso, S., Roehikepartain, E. Eds. (2006). *Nurturing Child and Adolescent Spirituality: Perspectives from the World's Religious Traditions*. Lanhan MD: Rowman & Littlefield.

2

Scriptural Understandings of Spirituality

Introduction

The previous chapter surveyed a variety of perspectives of spirituality, some Christian, but much contemporary scholarship in the field of spirituality is non-religious in its worldview, that spirituality is an innate and universal human characteristic, which can be studied through many academic disciplines. This chapter seeks to provide a specifically Christian perspective, as it affects Christian religious education and children's ministry. This is by presenting a theological perspective, and some scriptural understandings of spirituality, in particular, our understanding of the Holy Spirit, and the effect of the Holy Spirit on human lives. It also focuses on the need for those of us in children's ministry to be open to the Holy Spirit's influence in nurturing our own faith and making us effective in the work to which God has called us.

The term "spirituality" in the modern sense, as explored in the previous chapter, is not used in scripture. However a search of scripture reveals many references to the Spirit of God, or the Holy Spirit, and references to God's spirit as found in the created world and in human beings. So far we have concentrated on spirituality from a human perspective, but scripture approaches spirituality from the other direction. It begins with God.

Old Testament understandings of spirit

Christians are accustomed to references to the Holy Spirit, as coming upon the believers at Pentecost, and as the presence of God in the life of believers today. But according to the Old Testament, the Spirit of God has been there from the beginning, from eternity. In the first chapter of Genesis we read that "the Spirit of God moved upon the face of the waters" (Gen 1:2. KJV), or "a wind from God swept over the face of the waters" (NRSV – the translation to which I normally refer). In the Old Testament the Hebrew word *ruach* can mean wind, breath or spirit. For explanation of the word *ruach* I am referring to the Biblical scholar and theologian, Jürgen Moltmann (1992). Moltmann explained that the meaning of the word changed somewhat over time. Originally it probably represented the sound of a gale of wind, such as the wind that divided the Reed Sea during Israel's exodus from Egypt ((Ex. 14:21). When *ruach* is applied to God it is always something living and powerful. This is how the NRSV translates *ruach* in Genesis 1:2 as "a wind from God (that) swept over the face of the waters". *Ruach* also came to refer to "the breath of life and the power to live enjoyed by human beings and animals" (1992, p. 41), so that when animals die "the dust returns to the earth as it was, and the breath returns to God who gave it" (Eccles. 12:7). Psalm 104 is a hymn of praise to God for all his creation. It says of the animals:

> These all look to you to give them their food in due season:
> when you give to them, they gather it up:
> when you open your hand they are filled with good things.
> When you hide your face, they are dismayed:
> when you take away their breath (ruach), they die
> and return to their dust.
> When you send forth your spirit (ruach), they are created
> and you renew the face of the earth (Psalm 104: 27-30).

This is the sense of the reference in Genesis 2:7 where "the Lord God formed man from the dust of the ground, and breathed into his nostrils the breath of life: and the man became a living being" ("living soul" KJV). This life-giving presence of God is without limit and found everywhere human beings journey (Edwards, 2004, p. 36).

> Where can I go from your spirit?
> Or where can I flee from your presence?
> If I ascend into heaven you are there:
> if I make my bed in Sheol you are there ... (Ps. 139: 7,8).

It is this life-giving presence of God's spirit in human beings which enables them to respond to God. Job is reminded by his friend Elihu that "truly it is the spirit in a mortal, the breath of the Almighty that makes for understanding" (Job 32: 8).

In the Old Testament, *ruach* can be used in a number of other senses. It sometimes refers to a good spirit, or an evil spirit such as tormented King Saul (1 Sam 16:14). Spirit can refer to an attitude. In the book of Numbers is the story about the spies who did not have faith that God could enable Israel to conquer the promised land. One of the spies was Caleb who had a living faith in God. God says "But my servant Caleb, because he has a different spirit and has followed me wholeheartedly, I will bring into the land into which he went, and his descendents shall possess it" (Num 14: 24).

In the Old Testament "spirit" is also a special gift or anointing with power and authority for a God-given role. When Moses appointed seventy elders to help him administer justice among the people, God is quoted as saying ... "I will take some of the spirit that is on you and put it on them; and they shall bear the burden of the people along with you" (Num 11:17). Joshua had the spirit in both of these senses, of a right attitude and an anointing. At the end of his life Moses asked "the God of the spirits of all flesh" to appoint someone to lead the people after his death. Moses was commanded to take Joshua "a man in whom is the spirit", and consecrate him as the future leader (Num 27). Similarly, when the prophet Elijah was about to depart, his successor Elisha asked him, "Please let me inherit a double share of your spirit" (2 Kings 2:9). "Double share" of the spirit is not intended to imply that the spirit is a material substance that can be given out in portions, but that Elisha was to be appointed Elijah's heir, and an heir, or first-born son, was normally given a double portion of the family inheritance. The term is applied figuratively.

The conferring of the spirit for a special task was ritualised in the anointing of the kings of Israel, beginning with King Saul (I Sam 10). From King David's time this special endowment with the spirit gave anointed kings a special father/son relationship to God and a promise of a lasting, messianic kingdom (Moltmann, 1992, p. 43). This is illustrated in the messianic Psalm 2: 7b "You are my son: today I have begotten you." This theme of messianic anointing by the spirit of God is taken up in the various messianic passages in Isaiah: for example,

> The spirit of the Lord God is upon me,
> because the Lord has anointed me:
> he has sent me to bring good news to the oppressed,
> to bind up the broken hearted,
> to proclaim liberty to the captives,
> and release to the prisoners;
> to proclaim the year of the Lord's favour ... (Isaiah 61:1,2a).

An earlier passage in Isaiah points out that in the messianic kingdom there will not only be justice and peace in human society but the spirit will also bring new fruitfulness and blessing to the whole of creation, when "a spirit from on high is poured out on us, and the wilderness becomes a fruitful field, and the fruitful field a forest" (Is 32: 15).

The prophets looked forward to a time when all the nation of Israel would be made alive by the Spirit. In the well-known passage in Ezekiel chapter 37, the prophet had a vision of a valley of dry bones which came alive, when the wind, or breath, of God "came into them, and they lived, and stood on their feet, a vast multitude" (Ezek 37: 10). The prophet Joel, extends the promise of the coming of the spirit to bring new life even further, to a time, in the "last days", when "I will pour out my spirit on all flesh" (Joel 2:28), to include not only prophets and kings, but male and female, old and young, and even slaves. The apostle Peter claimed that this prophecy was fulfilled at the day of Pentecost (Acts 2:16ff).

Summary

The Old Testament presents a picture of the Spirit as breath, or life-giver, who was present at the beginning of creation, and is present as the source of life in all living things, particularly human kind. Human beings can respond to God by a right spirit of faith. Certain people, leaders, kings and prophets were anointed by the Spirit for the special task of leading the people of Israel. However, the presence of the Spirit was always available to breathe new life into all of his people, and to restore nations to peace and just living. This promise of new life in a messianic age also extended to all of creation, as illustrated in the picture in Isaiah chapter 11 of the wolf living with the lamb, and all creation being at peace.

Application to religious education

(a) Creator Spirit

In recent times there has been renewed interest among Christians, as well as the secular community, in our relationship with the environment and our role as custodians of God's creation. This chapter has explored the biblical concept of the Spirit as Breath of

Life for humanity and all creation. "When you sent forth your spirit they are created, and you renew the face of the ground" (Ps 104:30). Denis Edwards points out that:

> the Spirit is to be seen as Creator and Life-Giver, not just in the sense of biological life but in the wider sense of being the one who brings a universe to life. The Big Bang itself, the emergence of the great hydrogen clouds of the early universe, the cooking of carbon and the other elements in stars, the formation of our solar system – all of this is the work of the Life Giver" (Edwards, 2004, p.118).

Children are awe-struck by the wonders of creation. Alex, in my study, was one of the children who loved to speculate about the beginnings of the earth and its creatures. This fascination gives teachers of religious education a point of contact for introducing God as Creator, and his Spirit as the preserver of life. Most of the children in my study who discussed creation were willing to accept the concept of a Creator, and a meaning and purpose in creation. Some children in my research, like Jordan, had become convinced that the universe happened "by accident" but they were still willing to discuss the wonders of the universe and the earth. Contemporary children are concerned about the state of this planet, global warming and environmental degradation. They are particularly concerned about animals, and the fate of endangered species. Memorably, nine year old Ryan said "I don't believe in God, but I hate what people are doing to his planet". Some children saw looking after the planet and its creatures as a moral responsibility to God as the Creator, a responsibility shared by the whole human community.

> Caleb said "I reckon we should care for the birds because God created them to make us respect all living creatures and animals. And we should give lots of animals water to help them survive as well as us. With the birds, we can also take care of them, like, if they don't know where they are

> going... like they might fly into a tree or get injured, we can take them to the vet."
>
> When asked who might be "in charge of the universe", Caleb's response was "we are all in charge of the universe, and other people are living here in community too".

Another implication of the realisation that God's Spirit is everywhere as the Breath of Life in every human being and all creatures, is that children are already spiritual beings, capable of responding to God's invitation to a deeper relationship with him. This assertion is backed up by research, such as Hay and Nye's (2006) findings that children have a special sensitivity which they call Relational Consciousness. This phenomenon can be described as Consciousness in that children have a distinctive awareness of the world around them which generates a sense of wonder and delight, and "fosters a new dimension of understanding, meaning and experience (of meta-consciousness) in itself" (2006, p. 109). This sense is Relational in that this form of awareness heightens their sense of relationship to themselves, others, the world around them, and the Transcendent or God. In my own research this heightened sense of spiritual reality was expressed by the children in their relationships with others – the natural world, their relationships with family and friends, and their sensitivity to the mysteries of life. It was also expressed in their reflection on the meaning of their own lives, or their identity, and in the values for living that they developed out of their experiences of the special relationships in their lives.

Children already have a sense of the wonder and mystery of life which can be directed towards reflecting on God. They already have a sense of the importance of relationships with family and friends, which can be a basis for encouraging relationships with God. They already have a sense of morality, of what is really important in life, which can be a stepping stone to reflection on their own shortcomings, and the wonder of Christ's offer of salvation. It is true that, particularly for older children, this spiritual sensitivity is undermined by wider social influences, such as the decline in religious adherence, and the focus on individualism and materialism in Western society. Hay (2000) observed that by the time children reach the age of ten they are embarrassed by their own spiritual awareness. Retrospective studies of adults confirm that childhood spiritual experiences are often repressed or forgotten, but may be re-awakened in later life (Robinson, 1977). Hay (2000) sees the task of religious education as twofold: to nurture children's natural spiritual disposition, and to provide a class environment where it is safe to explore their spirituality, an environment which values shared community above isolated individualism.

(b) Anointing with the Spirit

The Old Testament gives many examples of people being endowed with the spirit for special vocations, such as military leader, prophet or king. This is a reminder to us as children's ministers or religious education teachers that, following the first disciples, we are called upon to be witnesses for Jesus Christ, who has promised us "power from on high" (Luke 24:29) for the task. We are promised the power and blessing of the Holy Spirit for our ministry in Christ's name.

The Holy Spirit in the New Testament

The adjective "spiritual" (*pneumatikos* in Greek) occurs frequently in the New Testament, particularly in Paul's writing, referring to "that which belongs to, or pertains to the Spirit" (Guthrie, 2011, p, xv). For Paul, a "spiritual person" is a "person of the Holy Spirit". Understanding spirituality in the life of the Christian arises from an understanding of the person of the Holy Spirit, whose work is to make and re-make our humanity in God's work of creation, incarnation and redemption. The Holy Spirit is the humanising Spirit (2011, p, xvi). We have already introduced the Hebrew word *"ruach" (pneuma* in Greek) which describes the living, unpredictable and mysterious nature of the Holy

Spirit. John's gospel expresses it this way: "The wind (*pneuma*) blows where it chooses, and you hear the sound of it, but you do not know where it comes from or where it goes. So it is with everyone who is born of the Spirit" (John 3:8). Although the Holy Spirit is mysterious and, in a sense, unknowable, he is known in the life of the Christian through his work of giving understanding, knowledge, guidance and speech. Jesus promised that the Spirit "will guide you into all truth' (John 16:13). Paul wrote to the Corinthians that the Holy Spirit would teach them true wisdom (1Cor. 2: 13), and give them gifts of "utterance", of wisdom and knowledge (1 Cor. 12:8). This new power to communicate the good news was demonstrated dramatically on the day of Pentecost. Even today Christians express the life of the Spirit in love and worship. As an early Church leader, Gregory of Nazianzus, declared "It is the Spirit in whom we worship and through whom we pray" (quoted in Guthrie, 2011, p. 15). All these features of the Holy Spirit, presented in the New Testament, indicate that the Holy Spirit is not an impersonal force, but a personal Spirit, who cannot be understood just through definitions and theological statements, but is known as a person is known, being both mysterious yet known in an intimate way through communication and worship (Guthrie, 2011).

The coming of Jesus, Son of God

The Life-giving Spirit of God had an important role in life and ministry of Jesus Christ. Ambrose, an early church leader, referred to the Holy Spirit as "the author of the Lord's incarnation (coming in the flesh)" (Edwards, 2004). The Apostle's Creed affirms that Jesus was "conceived by the Holy Spirit". This was affirmed in the message to Joseph in Matthew's gospel, and to Mary in Luke's gospel. "Even before Jesus appears on the scene, his saving mission is described in terms of the Spirit" (Edwards, 2004, p. 66). John the Baptist declared that Jesus would be the one promised by the prophets, to "baptise you with the Holy Spirit" (Mark 1:8), The gospel writers marked the arrival of the new era of the Spirit at Jesus' baptism with three symbolic events. The heavens were "torn apart", a sign of a new communication between heaven and earth. The Spirit descended "like a dove", reminiscent of the hovering of the wind of God at creation in Genesis chapter 3. And the voice from heaven declared "you are my Son, the Beloved, with you I am well pleased", which echoed Psalm 2:7 "You are my son; today I have begotten you". This marked the new beginning of the Kingdom of Heaven, or the age of the Messiah promised by the Old Testament prophets. Note that the Father, the Son (in the person of Jesus), and the Holy Spirit were all present and involved in Jesus' baptism. This is one basis for our belief in God as Trinity.

After his baptism the Spirit then "drove" Jesus out into the wilderness (Mark 1:12), where his temptations prepared him for his contests with Satan, and for his ministry of healing and preaching. Luke wrote that after the temptations "Jesus, filled with the power of the Spirit, returned to Galilee" and "began to teach in their synagogues and was praised by everyone" (Luke 4: 14-15). John's gospel introduced Jesus as the Word made flesh (John 1:14), and the one in whom the Spirit "abides" or "remains" (John 1:32, 33). John's gospel goes on to say that God (the Father) has sent the Son, and endowed him with the Spirit "without measure" (John 3:34). The gospels affirm that in the power of the Spirit Jesus drove out demons, healed the sick, received sinners, and brought the good new of his new kingdom to the poor. The Spirit was involved in every aspect of the life of Jesus. It follows that we, as Christians, need the involvement of the Spirit in every part of our lives too.

Jesus' mission as God's anointed one (Messiah or Christ) inevitably led to his suffering, death and resurrection. In this climax of his mission he continued to be led and sustained by the Spirit. Hebrews 9:14 tells us that, as a perfect sacrifice for humanity, he "through the eternal Spirit offered himself without blemish to God". Moltmann followed Mark's gospel in his explanation of the role of the Spirit in the passion (death and resurrection) of Jesus. Mark's passion story began at Gethsemane, where Jesus faced his coming suffering with a prayer to "Abba, Father", acknowledging his special relationship of Sonship to God. This is now the same address that Christians are able to make to God, as Father, in the Spirit (Rom 8:15 and Gal 4:6). Moltmann interpreted Jesus' statement that "the spirit is indeed willing but the flesh is weak" (Mark 14:38) as a contrast between the weakness of the disciples, and the power of the Spirit that rested on him, and enabled him to follow the Father's will even to death (1992, p. 64). Jesus felt that God the Father was hidden from him during his crucifixion, for he cried "My God, my God, why have you forsaken me?" (Mark 15:34), but the Spirit was with him in his suffering and death as "the power of an indestructible life" (Heb 7:16). "On Golgotha the Spirit suffers the suffering and death of the Son, without dying with him" (1992, p. 64). The dying Jesus "breathed his last" (Mark 15:37), or "gave up his (human) spirit" (John 19:30), but God raised him to life through the power of the Spirit, who is now "poured out" on all believers (Acts 2:32, 33).

> The resurrection involves a new and ultimate stage in the union between the humanity of Jesus and the Spirit, so that from this profound union the risen Christ sends the Spirit upon his disciples ... Jesus, who was Son of God in his life and death as Servant of God, becomes in his resurrection the firstborn of many Spirit-filled sons and daughters (Edwards, 2004, p. 81).

Summary

The Holy Spirit was active in every aspect of Jesus Christ's ministry, and his death and resurrection. The same Spirit is now active in the community of the church, and in individual Christians. Just as the Spirit was an "essential" part of Christ's life, so also the Spirit is necessary to the renewed life of Christians.

The Holy Spirit in the lives of Christians

Paul's letters have much to say about the quality of life "in the Spirit". Those who believe and who are baptised have received the Spirit in a special way. Paul tells us that "God's love has been poured into our hearts through the Holy Spirit that has been given to us (Rom. 5:5b). In Romans chapter 8 we are told that "the Spirit of God dwells in you" (Rom 8:9b) and that the Spirit bears "witness with our spirit that we are children of God" (Rom 8: 16). The Holy Spirit gives us many blessings, including wisdom and powers of discernment (1Cor. 2:15), gifts for ministry (1 Cor. 12:1-11), and the fruits of the Spirit (such as love, joy peace, patience ... self-control). These are demonstrated in our lives if we allow them to be continually guided by the Spirit (Gal. 5:22-25). Paul often warns his readers not to allow themselves to be driven by unworthy desires and aspirations of the world around them ("the flesh"), but to live "according to the Spirit", for "to set the mind on the flesh is death, but to set the mind on the Spirit is life and peace" (Rom. 8: 6). As children's ministers it is our privilege and responsibility to "set the mind on the Spirit" in our daily lives, and in our preparation and ministry to the children.

The Holy Spirit, as a member of the Trinity

This might be a good point to briefly explore what is meant by the Trinity, since this is a puzzle to teachers and to children. In a previous section Jesus was described as sent by God as Messiah to bring a new kingdom or salvation to the world. He was acknowledged as God's Son, and anointed with power by the Holy Spirit in his birth, baptism, ministry, death and resurrection. He was raised to a new life as exalted Son of God, and he has sent the Holy Spirit on all believers. God as Father, Son and Holy Spirit were involved in all stages of the life, death and resurrection of Jesus.

Christians believe that God is one divine Being but is known in three distinct "persons": Father, Son and Holy Spirit. We use many titles and analogies to describe the persons of the Trinity, and their relationships to one another, but human language cannot adequately define this mystery. Edwards (2004), based on the great fourth century church leader, Basil of Caesarea, used the titles Source of All, Word of God, and Breath of God for the Father, Son and Holy Spirit respectively. Some Christians use the titles Creator, Redeemer and Sanctifier, but this can be misleading because each member of the Trinity is involved in creation, redemption and sanctification. While people struggle to understand the divine mystery, the church from earlier times has used the formula "in the name of the Father, the Son and the Holy Spirit" in baptism (see Matt. 28: 19) and in worship. It is the way we experience God. In recent times Christian thinkers have renewed the emphasis of the early church on the idea of God as Trinity that expresses the communion of love within the godhead. This understanding is found in the gospels. For example Jesus is described by the Father as "my beloved Son", and Jesus claimed to do only the Father's will (John 5:19ff), and to love the Father (John 14:31). The intimate relation within the Trinity is also expressed when Jesus promised to send "the Advocate, the Holy Spirit, whom the Father will send in my name" (John 14: 26).

Again I refer to Moltmann, who describes the Trinity, not just in the traditional terms of the Father, the Son and the Holy Spirit as being three "persons" united in one "substance", but as persons in a special relationship of love.

> Every divine Person exists in the light of the other and in the other. By virtue of the love they have for one another they ex-ist (sic) totally in the other: the Father ex-ists by virtue of his love, as himself entirely in the Son, the Son, by virtue of his self-surrender, ex-ists as himself totally in the Father, and so on. Each Person finds his existence and his joy in the other Person (Moltmann, 1980. p. 173).

Theologians use the term *"perichoresis"* to describe "the living fellowship of the three Persons who are related to one another and exist in one another" (Moltmann, 1981. 175). Human beings are invited to share in this divine love which was demonstrated in the Father sending the Son into the world for our salvation.

> This union-communion-perichoresis opens outwards: invites human beings and the whole creation to insert themselves in the divine life: (as Jesus prayed) "May they be one in us ... that they may be one as we are one" (John 17: 21-22). (Boff, 1988, p. 6).

Christians are called to "image" the union-communion of the Trinity in their lives and their churches and community, by the power of the Spirit. Then we will be effective in our ministry.

> Their **imaging** of the Trinity is the gift of God's movement out of the circumference of the Trinitarian life to create human beings and, after they have sinned, to restore them by dwelling within them and taking them into the perfect communion of love, which God is ... (therefore we are called to) let ourselves be indwelled by God and to celebrate and proclaim what God has done, is doing, and will do (Volf, 2006, p. 6).

Summary

Christians have come to understand from scripture and reflection, that God is one, but known in three persons. Each person is distinct, and each is intimately related to the other in a communion of love. Christians are invited to share in the Divine communion of love, and to "image" or mirror this communion of love to others in the world.

Application

(a) The role of the Father through the Spirit in the life of Jesus Christ, Son of God, has a profound application for ordinary Christians, as the people who are called to carry on his ministry, to be his church. On a personal level Christians are also called upon, to do God's will and to love God. This is signified in the anointing of our baptism "in the name of the Father, the Son and the Holy Spirit". As children's ministers or religious education teachers we are anointed by the Trinity through the Holy Spirit to be witnesses of God's love to the children we meet. This is an awesome responsibility. But we are not working on our own, but through the power of the Holy Spirit. Therefore we can have faith that, through our ministry, the Holy Spirit will, in his own good time, call children to faith, and bring about the fruits of the Spirit (Galatians ch. 5) in the lives of the children in our care.

(b) The realisation that God, as Trinity, can be understood as a "communion of love" also helps us to understand what it means to be truly human. Firstly, God is understood as individual "Persons" in unity.

> The unity of the Godhead does not arise through negating the distinction between Father, Son, and Spirit, but rather through the mutual indwelling of Father, Son, and Spirit. Father, Son and Spirit act and have their being in and through one another (Guthrie, 2011, p. 83).

This individuality in communion, or community, is reflected in humanity, which was created in the image of God. In Genesis chapter 1 and 2, this "image of God" is complete when humanity is created male and female, a community of people. The Garden of Eden represents complete communion and harmony between the man and the woman and God. Although this harmony was lost, God through Christ has made peace with everything by "the blood of his cross". He has reconciled former enemies to himself and to each other.

"And through him (Christ) God was pleased to reconcile to himself all things, whether on earth or in heaven, by making peace through the blood of his cross" (Col 1: 20). He has created in himself "one new humanity" from groups of people who were once alienated from each other (see Eph. 2: 14-16).

This "new humanity" is able to fulfil the aspirations of modern spirituality: to reach a state of communion, or connectedness with God, nature, other people and the Self, which Hyde (2008) and others refer to as "Ultimate Unity". This unity is open to us as RE teachers and to our students, through the indwelling of the Holy Spirit. This is because we can be re-created in the "image" of a God who is a Trinity of love.

With these thoughts in mind, as children's ministers and RE teachers, we can be encouraged to be "steadfast, immovable, always excelling in the work of the Lord, because you know that in the Lord your labour is not in vain" (1 Cor. 15:58).

References

Boff, L. (1988). *Trinity and Society*. Tr. P. Burns. Maryknoll, NY: Orbis.

Edwards, D. (2004). *Breath of Life: A Theology of the Creator Spirit*. Maryknoll, NY: Orbis.

Guthrie, S. (2011). *Creator Spirit: The Holy Spirit and the Art of Being Human*. Grand Rapids, MI: Baker Academic.

Hay, D. (2000), Spirituality versus individualism: Why we should nurture relational consciousness. *International Journal of Children's Spirituality*, 5 (1), 37-48.

Hyde, B. (2008). *Children and Spirituality: Searching for Meaning and Consciousness*. London: Jessica Kingsley.

Moltmann, J. (1981). *The Trinity and the Kingdom of God*. Tr. M. Kohl. London: SCM.

Moltmann, J. (1992). *The Spirit of Life: A Universal Affirmation*. (Tr. M. Kohl). London: SCM.

Robinson, E. (1977). *The Original Vision: A Study of the Religious Experience of Childhood*. Oxford: The Religious Experience Research Unit.

Volf, M. (2006). Being as God is. *God's life in Trinity*. Eds. M. Volf & M. Welker, Minneapolis: Fortress Press.

Part 2

Introducing the Research

In the last two decades there has been increased interest in spirituality, and children's spirituality in particular. A number of books have been written, from the point of view of research, or of practical concern about Christian Education in schools, and nurture of children's faith in the home and in the church. These works have emanated mainly from The United States, the United Kingdom, Canada, and Australia. Part 2 of this book relates to research in children's spirituality.

The following chapters focus on the findings of my recent research, which examined children's spirituality from the context of Australian children who attended state primary schools. These children were nearly all from non-religious family backgrounds so their spirituality is generally not expressed in religious terms, but draws on the Australian natural environment, secular Australian culture, and the multi-national mass media. This section of the book examines the way the children in my research used these influences to fuel and express their innate spirituality. Using the findings of this research, and long experience as a classroom teacher and a Christian religious education teacher, in the next sections of the book I seek to address some of the practical issues of nurturing the spirituality of children in the classroom in the 21st century secular society.

Below is a summary of the main research and the concepts which shaped my research project. This material is rather technical, but is intended to provide a greater understanding of the descriptions of children's spiritual stories in the following four chapters. If the reader does not wish to follow this material, just proceed to Chapter 5.

Literature Review

The pioneering research of David Hay and Rebecca Nye (2006) has influenced a number of later authors. They started with a provisional set of interrelated categories of sensitivity or awareness: awareness-sensing, mystery-sensing, and value-sensing. Analysing conversations with 38 children in state primary schools in UK, they found in the midst of much everyday conversation there were some passages in the data which reflected a level of spiritual awareness which they called "Relational Consciousness". "Consciousness" referred to "something more than being alert and mentally attentive", which, in certain contexts, "fostered a new dimension of understanding, meaning, and experience" (2006, p.109). These special conversations were "Relational" in including more than relationships of "I-Others", and included also "I-Self", "I-world", and "I-God" in a special sense of awareness that added value to the children's everyday perspective (p. 109).

In the United States, Tobin Hart (2003) and his colleagues interviewed hundreds of children about their, often secret, spiritual experiences. Hart classified children's unique spiritual capacities as follows:

- *Wisdom*: a way of knowing and being, that takes small children beyond the limits of ordinary, everyday experiences into a deeper stream of consciousness where they are able to connect with people beyond the limits of time and space (p. 45).
- *Wonder*: experiences that can involve feelings of awe,

connection, joy, insight, and a deep sense of reverence, unity and love (p. 48).
- *Relationship*: refers to the compassion and sensitivity to the needs of others that is often displayed by young children (p.68).
- *Wondering*: refers to young children's capacity to consider questions of ultimate concern (such as questions about infinity, God and death) because of their openness, vulnerability and tolerance for mystery (p. 92).
- *Seeing the Invisible*: This includes altered states of consciousness which some young children experience, such as seeing angels, or aura around people, or expressing a more intuitive way of knowing than is usually expressed by older people (p. 116).

Hart's categories were incorporated into my research.

Brendan Hyde (2008) had a direct influence on my research model and the analysis of my findings. Hyde interviewed 36 children aged 8 and 10 in three Australian Catholic schools. His use of videotaped group interviews, and some of his stimulus material were followed in my research. His interviews made use of Hay and Nye's (2006) categories of *awareness sensing, mystery sensing,* and *value sensing,* and their concept of Relational Consciousness, in designing his interviews. Hyde's research analysis led him to define four subcategories of spiritual experience of Relational Consciousness as follows:

- *The felt sense*: awareness of surrounding time and space, and other people through immediate bodily sensations of touch, sight etc.
- *Integrating awareness*: where a child could be occupied with an immediate physical task, but at the same time engage in a higher level of consciousness required to hold a conversation with others.

- *Weaving the threads of meaning:* involved drawing on a number of sources of meaning (e.g. from home, school, church, public media) to attempt to create a unified worldview.
- *Spiritual questing:* involved "seeking to explore new and perhaps more authentic ways of connecting with Self, others, the earth and, for some, with God" (Hyde, 2008, p. 138).

The first two categories which Hyde produced were reflected in my research categories of Consciousness and Relationality. The third and fourth categories were mirrored in my research as Values and Identity, to be explained below.

Introducing my research

This research was influenced by these authors, and many others, including Elaine Champagne (2003), who introduced the concept of *Spiritual modes of being: Sensitive, Relational and Existential,* as mentioned in chapter 1. The aim of my recent research was to investigate the spirituality of children in Victorian state primary schools. The method involved semi-structured interviews with 24 children aged 8 to 10 in three schools: in a provincial city, a small rural community, and a Melbourne suburban school with a high migrant enrolment. This was preceded by preliminary interviews with four children at a coastal school. Meetings 1 and 2 were group interviews, and Meeting 3 was with individual children. The interviews were as follows:

Meeting 1 – Consciousness

Phase 1 – wondering

Activities – choose a photo of something amazing – spread out on table for selection

Possible questions – Why did you chose this picture? Tell us what you find amazing or unusual.

What does it make you think about?

What do the rest of you think about X's picture?

If you haven't chosen a picture, could you tell us about something amazing for you?

What is the most amazing or weird thing that has happened to you? Perhaps you haven't told anybody about it before.

Have you had a really amazing or weird dream?

Who is an amazing person for you?

Phase 2 – The Big question – introduce the title with a cue card.

Activity – show the picture of the thinking child.

Possible questions – What is this child thinking?

What is the biggest question you can think of?

Is there something you have always wanted to know? Who could you ask?

Is there a hard question you have figured out for yourself?

What do the others think of X's question? Have any of you got some ideas?

If you met someone in charge of the world/universe, (who might that be?) what question would you ask?

Meeting 2 – Relationality

Phase 1 – group activity – jigsaw puzzle – observe the interaction and strategies used.

Possible questions – Did you enjoy doing the puzzle? Why?

What things do you like doing with other people?

Who do you specially like doing things with?

Do you have a special place that you go with your friends? What do you do there?

Is there a special place where you like to go to be quiet and think, or do your special things?

Phase 2 – Read the story *The violin man*.

Possible questions – Did you like the story? Note the little pink creatures. What might they be?

Was Oscar a sad man or a happy person? What made him happy or sad?

Who were Oscar's friends? What did they do to be friends to him?

Does a friend have to be a person? Who are your friends? Do you have other kinds of friends?

Who were Oscar's family in the story? Did it matter to him that Marietta was dead?

What do you think happens when people are dead?

What do you think it would be like to have no living family around, like Oscar?

What is it like to be in a family? Who are the most important people in your life?

Which places were real (or familiar) for Oscar and which places were not so real for him?

What places are real or unreal for you?

What did Oscar dream about?

Do you have dreams or imagine something you would like to happen?

Meeting 3

Phase 1 – Identity (take drawing materials etc)

Activity – make a drawing of yourself, or a concept map of yourself and your world.

Possible questions – Tell me about your drawing. What does it say about you?

Are you different or the same as other people (your friends, siblings)?

Do you think that you are special in some way? What makes you special/different?

What do your family/friends think about you? Do you agree with them?

Could you tell me a story about something special that you do, or has happened to you?

Some people think of God as special. Who do you think of as special?

What things do you like to imagine?

Phase 2 – Roadmap

Activity – show the picture of the Kosovo refugees. Explain the picture as necessary.

Possible questions – What is happening to these people? Where are they going?

What could be done to help them?

Is there anything you could do to help them? Tell me about a time when you helped somebody.

Has anybody helped you?

What are some good things that people do? What are some bad things that people do?

If you had 3 wishes for the world, or people you know, what would they be?

Activity – draw a picture of "Your Journey". It can be anything real or imaginary.

Tell me about your drawing.

What would you like to happen when you are a teenager, a grown-up?

Using a research method called "hermeneutic phenomenological research method", the material gathered from the videotaped interviews was transcribed, then analysed initially by preparing a spiritual profile of each child, using Champagne's (2003) spiritual *modes of being*. The model for structuring my research and further analysis of the research findings, represented in the diagram below, arose out of the literature on spirituality from various traditions and times, and recent research in children's spirituality.

Figure 1: A Conceptualization of the Dimensions of Spirituality

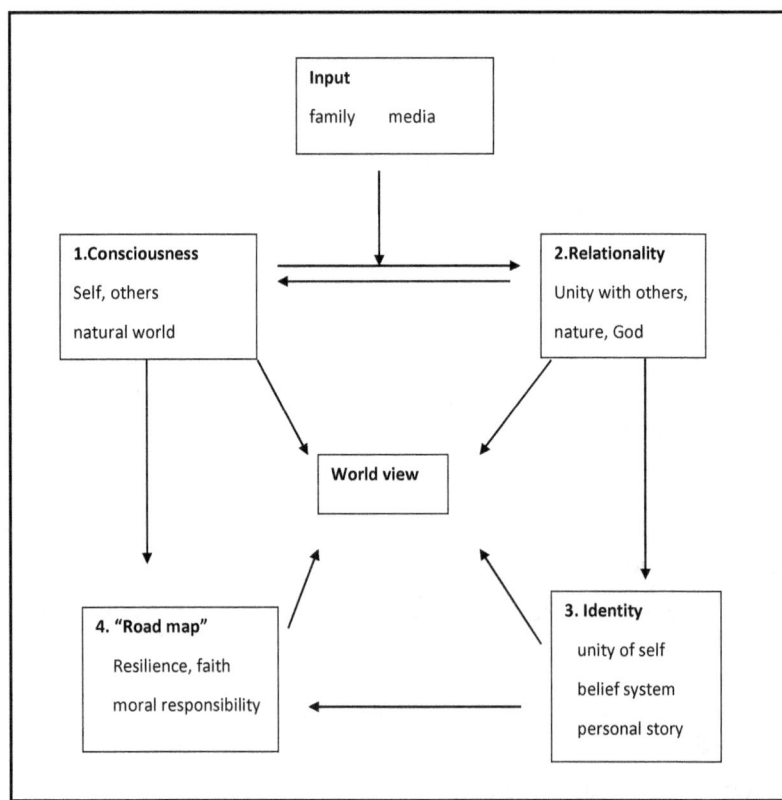

Explaining the Model

This model, illustrated in the diagram above, has the following four dimensions: a) Consciousness, b) Relationality, c) Identity, and d) Roadmap (Moriarty, 2010). These four dimensions, which were presumed to be complementary and at the core of children's spirituality, are represented as in equilibrium, and their presumed interconnection is represented by the two-way arrows. At the periphery of the diagram the various external influences on the development of children's spirituality, such as family and the media, are represented by the Input box. *Consciousness* refers to a heightened awareness of the spiritual in the world around, and in the transcendent world, whether one believes in a God or not. This consciousness is expressed as sensitivity to mystery and responses of awe and wonder. "*Relationality*" is a term which refers to relationship with Self, the world, other people and the transcendent. *Consciousness* (or sensitivity) and *Relationality* are often conceived of as a single dimension, for example, by Hay and Nye (2006). *Identity* refers to self-image or self-concept (an awareness of who we are). "*Roadmap*" refers to the values and aspirations which provide a moral compass and vision in a child's life. *Worldview* is represented centrally as a meaning-making factor which binds all the other factors together. This model, arising out of the literature, provided a useful method for structuring the research method and for analysing the research findings. The conclusion of the analysis led to a slightly modified model, based on some unexpected findings.

Spirituality as Multidimensional

While various authors emphasise a particular one of my dimensions of spirituality, for most of the authors reviewed, children's spirituality was conceived of as multidimensional. Hay and Nye (2006) noted that experience of Relational Consciousness is often expressed in moral values, as "when Freddie considered his religious views about creation, his personal conception of spiritual values (of relating positively to other children) was triggered" (p. 112).

Hart (2003) analysed children's spirituality under the headings of Listening to Wisdom, Wonder, Between you and me, Wondering, and Seeing the invisible. These categories not only cross the boundaries between Consciousness and Relationality, but also reflect the dimensions of Worldview, Roadmap and Identity. Hart noted that childhood moments of wonder "shape the way a child sees and understands the world, and they often form a core of his or her spiritual identity, morality, and mission in life" (p. 53).

Hyde's (2008) findings also suggest a multidimensional model. His characteristic of *Felt Sense* was roughly equivalent to Consciousness in my model, *Integrating Awareness* to Relationality, and *Weaving the Threads of Meaning*, and *Spiritual Questing* inspired the concepts of Roadmap and Identity.

Another major contributor to my model was Elaine Champagne (2003). Her *Spiritual Modes of Being*, namely *Sensitive, Relational and Existential*, not only helped to structure my conceptual model, but also aided me in detecting behavioural evidence of spirituality, which Champagne referred to as "keys", in the large quantity of research transcriptions.

The Modified Model

This diagram represents a more dynamic conceptualisation of children's spirituality than the original model, Figure 1. It suggests a circular, and possibly a spiral movement, representing a process rather than a state of being. Although the children in the study rarely spoke about their sense of identity, there was some evidence that identity formation developed out of experiences of heightened Consciousness, leading to enhanced Relationships and a sense of meaning or value, (Roadmap). This in turn seemed to lead to children

Figure 2. *A revised conceptualization of the dimensions of spirituality – emanating from the findings of this research*

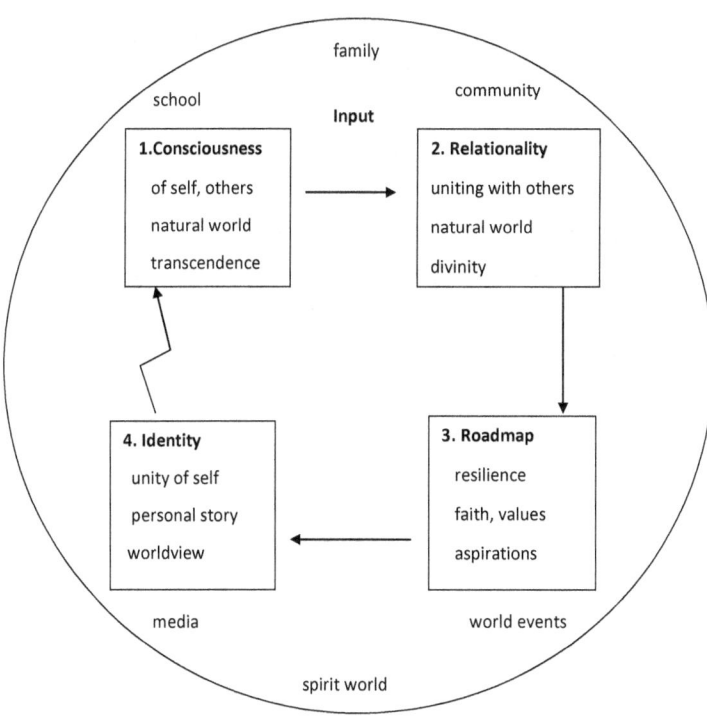

forming a sense of Self or Identity through the story of their lives, and possibly leads to a further level of heightened consciousness. This is represented by the one-way arrows in the diagram. External influences are represented as affecting spirituality at any point in the cycle. For these children, worldview seemed to be in the process of development, and part of Identity rather than a separate construct.

This conception of children's spirituality as a process of development rather than a state of being is consistent with the views of other writers. Hart (2003) defined spirituality as both a worldview (state of being) and a process of development. As a worldview it "located the individual in a multidimensional, sacred universe" (2003,

p. 9). As a process of development Hart perceived spirituality as "an ongoing growth process – a process of identity ... recognised as integration and wholeness" (2003, p. 9). Webster (2005) also recognised these two aspects of spirituality, when he stated that "personal identity is gained by *how* an individual relates to and values his or her relations" (2005, p. 9). Eaude (2005) proposed metaphors such as "growth, health, integration", suggesting that children can "regress as well as progress", but overall he saw spirituality as "a process, rather than a set of specific experiences" (2005, p. 245). This progression may provide some insight into the way in which the spiritual relationships with Self and Other are incorporated into a meaningful personal story.

References

Champagne, E. (2003). Being a child: A spiritual child. *International Journal of Children's Spirituality* 8 (1): 43-53.

Eaude, T. (2005). Strangely familiar? – Teachers making sense of young children's spiritual development. *Early Years* 25, (3): 237-248.

Hart, T. (2003). *The Secret Spiritual World of Children*. Makawao, HI: Inner Ocean.

Hay D. & Nye, R. (2006). *The Spirit of the Child*, (Rev. ed.). London: Jessica Kingsley.

Hyde, B. (2008). *Children and Spirituality: Searching for Meaning and Connectedness*. London: Jessica Kingsley.

Moriarty, W. (2011). A conceptualization of children's spirituality arising out of recent research. *International Journal of Children's Spirituality.* 16 (3): 271-285.

Webster, R. S. (2005). Personal identity: Moving beyond essence. *International Journal of Children's Spirituality,* 10, (1): 5-16.

3

REACHING BEYOND THEMSELVES:
CONSCIOUSNESS AND RELATIONALITY (1)

Introduction

This chapter reviews findings of my research which relate to children's spiritual capacity to view the world and what might lie beyond this world with a sense of awe and wonder. Tobin Hart, a Psychologist from the USA wrote, "Children are natural philosophers. Much to our amazement, they wonder about the big questions. They ask about life and meaning, knowing and knowledge, truth and justice, reality and death" (Hart, 2003, p. 91). This chapter demonstrates that at least some of today's children seek for connections with the natural world, with other people, and with God, or the realm beyond physical reality, which we call the Transcendent. Therefore this chapter is called "Reaching beyond themselves".

When I asked a group of children, "Who is in charge of the universe?" Mary replied,

> God, and Jesus (are in charge of the whole world). God made it, and Jesus his son, and he looks after it, if he's not dead. And if he is (dead) it's sad because when Jesus, God, dies he put his son in charge and if he had a daughter he put her is charge after Jesus dies, and he would put his wife in charge if the kids were dead ... Like the people have to get in charge and the people who made it. And I know the

first person who was actually born, the first person who died would make the whole world and the oldest person who died. That was God.

Although Mary's description of God seemed very confused at first sight, it reveals something of her concept of God. God made the whole world, or universe. God existed before anyone else. Like many children of her age, God and Jesus are interchangeable identities as well as distinct persons. How did Mary try to make sense of the mystery of who is "in charge"? Mary called on her own experience of family life, of family responsibility and care, and the reality of the recent death of her great grandmother. The parents are in charge, but when the parents get old and die, the grown up children take over responsibility for the family. Mary believed that God is Creator. He is in heaven, which is everywhere, so God is with us and taking care of us. Heaven is an important place for Mary, and most of the children I interviewed, as the place where loved family members go. Mary believed that her great grandmother is happy in heaven, in contrast with her last days on earth, when she could neither see nor hear. Death was a personal issue for Mary because she suffered from asthma and worried that she might die during an asthma attack. However her fear of death was that "I wouldn't be able to be with my family again, or play with them and do lots of stuff." While Mary had some sense of a relationship with God, the real, meaningful relationship was with her family, and her belief in God was based on that relationship.

Mary also described her experience of seeing an angel. She was aged 6, and was in hospital to have some teeth filled. When her mother and father left her overnight, she was feeling really scared. She said that suddenly an angel appeared and said "Don't be afraid. I'll stay with you tonight. I won't leave you tonight. And I'll be there with you tomorrow". She described the angel as wearing a gold dress and a bright thing on her head. She had wings. Although Mary only saw her briefly, she was aware that the angel was still present with her.

Significantly, Mary said "That night I wasn't scared". Although Mary was given to telling fanciful tales, I found this one credible, because of her deep fear of dying.

Tobin Hart noted that previously most psychologists, educators and religious leaders assumed that children are incapable of "direct and intimate connection with the Divine" (Hart, 2003, p. 3). However Hart's experience through his own children and extensive professional research led him to believe that children have a "capacity for wonder and wisdom, for compassion and deep questioning, and for seeing beneath the surface of the physical world" which is largely unacknowledged (p. 3). During my conversations with Mary I learned about her sense of wonder and her questioning about the nature of God and the mysteries of death and a realm beyond this life. She told me about her relationships with her family and friends, and her concern for the environment in her concern to save water for its creatures. And, as described above, she had a capacity to see beyond the physical world in her encounter with the angel.

However, this last capacity, which Hart (2003) called "Seeing the Invisible" was not mentioned by any other of the children I interviewed. It is significant that Mary saw the angel when she was aged 6, not 9, which was the age when she was interviewed. A number of writers have noted that children tend to keep secret, or even forget, their intense spiritual experiences as they get older because they are misunderstood or dismissed as fanciful by adults (Hart 2003). David Hay (2000) concluded that in contemporary society spirituality is considered a private matter by religious people, (and as "unscientific" by many non believers). According to Hay, "children are embarrassed by their own spiritual awareness, particularly by the time they reached the age of ten" (2000, p. 39). As the children in my research were reaching this age it was necessary to look elsewhere for evidence of their spirituality.

Reaching beyond themselves: relating to God or something Other.

Although not all the children in my research had a sense of the reality of God, they all had a sense of mystery, and seemed to be reaching towards a reality beyond their everyday experience. Hay and Nye (2006) identified this phenomenon as "a form of awareness, different from and transcending everyday awareness, which is potentially present in all human beings (Hay & Nye, 2006, p. 22).

The children in this present research used their sense of wonder about the natural world as a means by which to relate to Something Other. This was particularly true for the children at the suburban school, who expressed their sense of wonder through a language of science and technology. For them scientific ideas and discoveries can be a source of wonder. The following extracts, from the children's spiritual profiles were indicative of this feature.

> Harry wondered "How does the world stand up?" And he wondered about "the circle [sic] of humans and the generations". Harry wanted to know why coca cola fizzes when you drop a menthol sweet into it. He also watched his father repair the car, to see how the engine and the various tools work.

> Lucy's Big Questions were also about solving scientific problems. She wanted to know "how electrical things work, like you know, remote things? How does the car know what to do?" And why does an electric oven heat up slowly rather than instantaneously?

The children in this school expressed amazement at living creatures, especially small ones, a reaction which was in response to a picture of a newly hatched bird. They discussed what species of bird it might be, and how it could have fitted into the egg. They related their experiences of finding a sick bird, or eggs that had fallen out of the nest, and their efforts to care for them. Most of the children at each school were fascinated by small animals, and described them as "cute", "magical" and vulnerable. At the suburban school this extended to discussion about the wonder of human birth, which they had witnessed in their families or on television. Amanthi chose a picture of some people in Middle Eastern dress bending over a baby, which she interpreted as "the baby Jesus". Amanthi came from a Buddhist family which had recently arrived in Australia, but the picture had special spiritual significance for her because she had heard the Christmas and Easter stories in Christian religious education at school. She explained that Jesus "gave his life for us".

This material demonstrated Champagne's spiritual modes of being in a number of ways. Harry and Lucy were exercising the *sensitive mode* in their visual observations of what they saw in scientific phenomena, such as coca cola fizzing when menthol is dropped into it. The children in this group also used their skills of observation to decide the species of the newly hatched bird. However, they were doing more than just observing; they were exercising the *existential mode of being*. They were trying to discover the mysteries of how things work, such as a car engine, and the spiritual significance of physical phenomena, their deeper meaning. Harry not only wanted to know "How does the world stand up?" but how he fits into the grand mystery of "the circle of humans and the generations". This attitude of reverent awe was also demonstrated in their attitude to human birth as they had witnessed it personally or through pictures. Amanthi expressed this awe in religious terms when she related to the special significance of the birth of Jesus, as she understood it. These children also expressed their awe in a *relational mode*, when they associated the picture of the baby bird with past experience of trying to care for a baby bird, and their emotional response of describing the bird as "cute".

These children were demonstrating spirituality in that they were reaching beyond what they could observe, toward deeper mysteries of how the world "stands up", and their place within the "circle" of being. As Hart (2003) observed, "Children are natural philosophers. To our amazement, they often wonder about big questions... entertaining the big questions is a way to enter a dialogue with mystery, and with the spiritual" (p. 91). The children in this group related the mysterious to everyday relational experiences, such as caring for a baby bird, or watching a father repair a car. Amanthi, who loved baby birds and human babies, made a link between the picture of a baby and some understanding of the mystery of the Incarnation. These children seemed to be on the threshold of a theological understanding of transcendent reality and the seeds of faith. For faith has been described as "the conviction of things not seen ... (for) by faith we understand that the worlds were prepared by the word of God, so that what is seen was made from things that are not visible" (Hebrews 11:1, 2).

This material demonstrated children's spirituality through the *sensitive mode of being* in their heightened consciousness of the physical and the transcendent worlds. In asking philosophical questions they were engaging the *experiential* mode, or in *spiritual questing* (Horell, 2003; Hyde, 2008), in a contemporary post-modern world where there are a multiplicity of explanations for the mysteries of life, they were seeking new and authentic ways of connecting with self, others, the earth and God (Hyde, 2008).

The children at the provincial school reached beyond themselves, in both the *sensitive* and *existential modes*, in their fascination with beginnings, and the creation of the world, as demonstrated in this extract from Alex's profile.

> Alex described how land animals evolved as follows. "...a bit of the earth was joined together, and that cracked and there was this massive island, like a rock around the world, and that cracked, and then all these monsters, like, really weird dinosaurs just came out of the ocean, and they

formed into land ones". Or "maybe they were eggs and they floated up to the top, and maybe the wind blew them onto the land, and they just became dinosaurs." Although Alex didn't express a personal belief in God, he did not believe things just happened by accident, and offered these possible explanations. His explanation for the origin of the Australian aborigines was this. "Although they were just normal people from other countries and they came to Australia first, and maybe they walked into a swamp, and they got all muddy, and they just … walked back out, and they couldn't get the mud off, and they got dark."

Alex also had a sense of the "wholeness" of creation. He chose as an awesome picture a photograph of the earth from space. There was some response to the white patches in the photograph, which he interpreted as water, but his main interest was in the idea of representing the whole earth … "different people all over the world, different animals, different houses" and different kinds of electronic games which children might be able to exchange.

Alex's observations about the view of the planet from space was followed by a group discussion about sporting heroes, and about the recent death of Steve Irwin, an Australian media hero and crocodile hunter[4]. The children were all shocked by his death. In the following conversation quoted from the transcripts they reached beyond themselves in that they were wrestling with the meaning of Steve Irwin's death, and the really big questions of the origin of the universe, and how they fitted into the universal economy.

Alex: When I'm playing with my Play Station, I sometimes

---

4 Steve Irwin was an Australian conservationist, who operated a zoo for native animals, particularly crocodiles. He also made a number of wild life documentaries and televisions programs. His flamboyant personality and his propensity to push the boundaries of safety made him a hero to Australian children. He was killed by a stingray in 2006 while making an underwater documentary, shortly before these children were interviewed.

think 'life's a video game'. It's really strange. It's like aliens from other galaxies are controlling us.

Billy: I reckon it's aliens controlling us, us controlling the game, and the game's controlling, and it keeps on going.

W (Interviewer): Who started it all? Who do you think is controlling the universe?

Billy: God. I think God, because he made the universe.

Jordan: I don't believe in God. So I don't think he started it all.

W (to Jordan): Who (or what) do you think started it all?

Jordan: I don't know.

W: It just happened by accident perhaps?

Jordan: I think it was a bomb. (Jordan is well read in scientific literature.)

W: They say the universe started with a Big Bang, don't they?

Ruth had her hand up to speak: I don't think aliens are controlling us, or maybe I wouldn't be speaking right now, because I've got a brain.

W: You think you are controlling yourself?

Ruth: Yes.

Alex and his friends demonstrated each of the modes of being, in their exploration of existential questions concerning the earth and its origins through playful use of their imaginations (Hay & Nye, 2006, p. 121). Alex demonstrated the *sensitive mode* in his fascination with the picture of earth from space, in the earlier passage from his profile, where he concluded that the white patches were probably oceans. His imaginative explanations, in the text above, were full of visual images – massive island, monsters, dinosaur eggs, and aborigines walking into a muddy swamp. These images shaped his mode of being as demonstrated in his stories. Alex appeared to connect and communicate with the spiritual realm through his visual sense. In this regard he was *"incorporated* in the world" (Champagne, 2003, p. 46).

Alex revealed the *relational mode* as he studied the picture of the earth. In his imagination he related to "different people all over the world, different animals, different houses", and children playing electronic games, just like himself. Moreover, in this interview Alex and his friends became absorbed with existential questions. They were concerned with questions of time and the length of evolutionary time caused them wonderment. They wondered about the formation of the continents, the evolution of the dinosaurs, and the origin of the Australian aborigines. They were hazy about the dimensions of earth time, but agreed that the topics under discussion happened "before Christ".

The existential mode of place occupied them in that they could place themselves in space, looking at earth, but their base for perspectives on the world was Australia. Their relationship to existence was expressed in a number of ways. They were concerned with the origin and purpose of creation and human life. This conversation was again triggered by mention of the death of Irwin, the crocodile hunter. The group discussed whose fault it was that Irwin died. Was the stingray that killed him to blame or was Irwin responsible for his death by getting too close to the stingray? The question was not really resolved, but it did lead to the conversation, from the transcript, recorded earlier in the chapter, where Alex said "When I'm playing with my Play Station, I sometimes think 'life's a video game'". In this interview Ruth grappled with the concept of purpose. Later in the conversation, when the children were again discussing whether God created the universe or it happened "by accident" Ruth commented:

> Maybe there was an accident and an animal got turned

into a dinosaur. Maybe it was, like poison from something. And maybe that turned them into a dinosaur … I think, by accident. There's no point of them if they're just going to die out. (W: Why make them if they are not going to last?) Everyone's going to die.

More was revealed about Ruth's *existential mode of* being in extracts from her profile. Although Ruth did not openly express a belief in God, she seemed to be grappling with the concept of purpose. Ruth told a (true) story she saw in a movie, about a boy, who had "really, really short legs and he couldn't walk properly". This boy who was rejected by his parents, found meaning in his life when he was able to rescue someone from drowning, but died himself. Ruth explained that "The boy always thought that God had a special purpose for him, that he was meant to be like that because it was something special". This sense of purpose was complemented by her sense that as humans we are responsible for our actions. She did not accept the idea of being controlled by aliens. "I think we're controlling ourselves, because if aliens were controlling us then I wouldn't be speaking right now, because we've all got a brain". Ruth's two wishes demonstrated both her interest in scientific explanations, and the mystery of the transcendent. One wish was to know "What's up in heaven?" Her grandmother had recently died, and she believed that she was in heaven. Another wish was to know about individual differences. "How we look the way we are. Why is everyone different? How does it work? … How come you have glasses and I don't have glasses?" Ruth was revealing aspects of her spirituality in that she was seeking to make meaning in various transcendental mysteries, such as "Was there a divine purpose in the handicapped boy's life?" "Are we in control of our lives?" "What is heaven like?" and "Why are human beings so different from each other?"

Summary: Sense of wonder

The children who took part in this study demonstrated their spirituality through their sense of wonder in a number of ways. Some children at the suburban school expressed their wonder at the mysteries to be investigated through science and technology, that is, through their *sensitive mode*, like how heat is dispersed in an oven. They also expressed their sense of wonder at the mystery of living things, through their *relational mode* when they expressed their sense of wonder at small or newly born creatures. They also reached beyond themselves through their *existential mode*, as well as the other modes, when they discussed their experiences of human birth. For one child this was extended into a religious understanding of the mystery of the birth of Christ. Some children at the provincial school also examined the mysteries of the created world: the beginnings of the earth and its creatures. They explored the existential mysteries of a human perspective of interplanetary space and their place as members of the whole human race. They explored the mysteries of time: the beginnings of the earth and its creatures, including human beings. There was also discussion about the purpose of creation and human life: whether we are the victims of chance, controlled by outside forces ("life's a video game"), or whether there is an ultimate purpose in human life, even the life of a handicapped child. Ruth said, "I have a brain", therefore she believed that we have at least some control over our destiny. Some of the children, particularly Ruth, had a sense that there might be a heaven, and a God who cared about them.

The mystery of death

Death is an issue that almost universally raises questions of ultimate meaning: about what might lie beyond this life. The children at each school were interested in the mystery of death and what might happen after a person dies. Discussion about death was usually in the context of reviewing the book, *The Violin Man*, (Thompson, 2004). In this story Oscar continued to feel the presence in his life of his daughter, Marietta, who had died. The children told stories about the death of family members. Most of the children agreed that after a person died they lived on in the memories of those who loved them. Most had a vague idea that the soul or spirit went "up" to heaven, and the body decayed. Below are some extracts from the transcripts of a conversation between Alex, Billy, Jordan and Ruth, about what happened to people when they die.

> Ruth: Even if they leave you they can still be your friend because you've still got the memory of how they have been to you. My grandma died and went up to heaven. Like my grandmother died and she got cremated, because she died of cancer in her body, in her stomach, and it spread through all her body. She didn't want to go to hospital…About two years ago.
>
> Alex: I'm not really sure, maybe their spirits go up or something, and all their bones and stuff stay in the coffin.
>
> Billy: You can still talk to them. Their souls go up. I think. (after a pause) I've got a question. Do we actually turn into skeletons?
>
> Jordan: I know what happens to you. The worms go through the coffin, suck the air out of it. The body starts to dissolve (and eventually) they turn to skeletons. I found out in the encyclopaedia…It's got a picture of a real skeleton in it.

For a number of children, the mystery of death was the point at which they encountered the Transcendent and the possibility of religious faith, particularly if they had had the experience of a loved one who had died. In *The Violin Man* Oscar had no family except his daughter, Marietta who had died, but he continued to feel her presence with him. The children were asked "How could Marietta still be his 'friend' if she was dead?" And "What do you think happens to people when they die?" Some children also discussed death in their individual interviews, if someone important to them had died. Champagne's *modes of being* provided a useful tool for examining the phenomenon of death, as it affected their spirituality.

Some children engaged with death through their *sensitive mode*. Jordan was curious about death, although he did not mention anyone close to him who had died. He concentrated his curiosity on the physical aspects of death – how the body decays. This perspective could be expected in children, who perceive humanity in concrete physical ways, as a body they can see, touch and talk to. Therefore it could be expected that Jordan, who claimed to be an "atheist", would focus on the sensory aspects of death, or what can be physically observed. "For the atheist answers (to questions about spiritual mysteries such as death) are to be found in the immanent world of nature, rather than in an imaginary transcendent realm populated by divine beings" (Wright, 2000, p. 53).

Lucy, from the suburban school, had a mixture of reactions to death. Her first response was similar to the others in her group. To the question at the end of the reading of *The Violin Man*, "What do you think happens to people when they die?" Lucy replied, "I think the people who love them can actually see them in their imagination, and they still are there…" To a later question, "What happens to their 'souls'?" Lucy pointed upwards. These responses seemed to arise out of the theme of the story, and common Western views about heaven and hell, and not impinge on her directly. Here is an extract from her transcript, taken from a later individual interview.

> Lucy: I wish no-one would die, that everyone would just live for ever, and they never die.
>
> W: What do you think about dying?
>
> Lucy: I think it's very sad when someone close to you dies, as my grandma died. And before I was even born my grandpa died.

W: So you didn't know him?

Lucy: I've seen pictures of him though.

W: Have you been to his grave, in (her country of origin)?

Lucy: (shakes her head).

W: What do you think happens to people when they die?

Lucy: Our guide(?) says their spirit is still there. Like, they're still there, like a ghost, but I don't believe in ghosts. I just think, I just think like they're just gone. Like when they die they are not there any more.

In this extract Lucy responded in her *relational mode* in that she expressed sadness about her grandmother's death, and for the relationship she never had with her grandfather in the flesh. Hay and Nye (2006, p. 119) noted that children like Lucy commonly have a sense of kinship between the living and the dead. The children appreciated the sensory link through photographs of someone who had died. Lucy grappled with the existential meaning of death. She expressed angst about the general question of why people die, and humanity's longing for immortality. She also expressed scepticism about her community's religious belief in ghosts. In the earlier group interviews Lucy demonstrated a fascination with science and scientific method, which popularly finds no room for the supernatural. These extracts seemed to demonstrate the dilemma of some migrant children, in being torn three ways, between eastern and western religious beliefs, and a popular idea of scientific proof. Most of the children referred to in this discussion of their reactions to death did not have a close personal relationship with someone who had died, nor did they appear to have a belief in God or a sense of relationship with the transcendent. *Relational modes of being* which reach beyond the physical world, such as with a family member who has died, seem to make a difference to the quality of children's spirituality. It opened up for them the possibility of the reality of heaven, and a relationship with God.

Summary: The mystery of death

The children who took part in this study seemed to reach beyond themselves with regard to the mystery of death in three ways. Some exercised their *sensitive mode*, Jordan, for example, in concentrating with fascination on the decay of the body of the person who has died. Others, like Lucy, focused on the ongoing relationship with the deceased through the memories of the living. However, most of the children also had a sense of a transcendent dimension to death, whether as a soul that goes "up" to heaven, a "ghost" that remains, or, as discussed in a later section, as someone who is with God and still watching over the living. Beliefs about life after death seemed to be largely influenced by their cultural heritage. For most of these children, the two subjects in which they were willing to discuss God, or the transcendent, were death and creation.

Personal experiences of death

Kelly, from the provincial school, was another child who struggled to find a meaning in death, arising out of her personal experience. Kelly had conflicted relationships with her family, and her friends. The most significant relationship for Kelly was with her step-father, Pete, who died about 12 months previously of "sun cancer". (I got the impression that there had been several step-fathers in her life). She described Pete as "like a father" to her, who cared for her when she was sick. She described, on two occasions, how Pete got sick, and she visited him in the hospital, and gave him drinks and kept him company. She repeated that he was making good progress with his illness on "good medication", but the hospital changed it to "bad medication", and he died. In this explanation she seemed to be trying to understand the mystery of his death. Whenever she passed the hospital where he died she pointed out the window to his room, as though he was still there. She believed that Pete was in heaven, but somehow still nearby, "keeping watch over us wherever we go". She summed up how she felt about her present relationships as follows: "I'd rather be with Pete right now, in heaven and have a family, and see my great, great aunty, than be down here and get picked on".

Kelly was one of the few children who had a personal belief in God. She was very conscious of heaven, which she associated with her stepfather Pete, who had died, and was with God. "Heaven is actually the whole sky, everywhere, all the time. God is watching everyone, like all the relatives." She had a sense of the transcendent in which she was part of a cosmic family, of which God was the head. For Kelly, God was a benevolent being, who created the universe, and was "really, really good at it". She also had a sense of her own family extending across many generations, placing herself is a larger frame than her present dysfunctional family. She said "God created the whole world, our mums and dads, because he made Mummy's mum to have Mum. If my mum wasn't born I wouldn't be here right now".

Kelly did not have a very satisfactory relationship of trust with her family, with the exception of Pete, who had died. However, Pete's death strengthened her spirituality in a number of ways. Kelly's *relational mode of being* was strengthened in that she then had a sense of transcendent relationships which extended beyond this world, beyond time and place. That is, her relational experiences drew her into the *existential mode*. She felt that she belonged to a transcendental family which included God as head, and people like Pete and her great grandmother who had died. She then had a sense that her family in this world had a larger time scale extending across many generations, and members of each generation had a purpose in God's plan. This was illustrated when she said "If my mum wasn't born I wouldn't be here right now". This gave her a positive sense of identity, of being accepted as part of the great family, headed by an ever present, all powerful and loving God. Kelly's experience of the death of her stepfather seemed to be a spring-board to faith.

Reaching beyond themselves through relating to the earth, others and themselves

In examining children's significant "this world" relationships, further use is made of Champagne's (2003) three *modes of being*. The concept of the *relational mode* is developed further through the researcher's own categories of bonding, empathy and values formation, arising out of children's particular relationships with the natural world, their peers and families. "Bonding" is defined here as any "relationship in which people establish a strong emotional attachment to each other", and includes some of Champagne's descriptions such as affectionate, privileged, affirming, referencing, inclusive (p. 48-50). "Empathy" refers more to "mentally entering into the feeling or spirit of a person or thing", such as the feelings of a friend or stranger who is hurt, or other people's happiness. "Values formation" has some parallels in Champagne's work, such as "forgiving, affirming, internalising". In this book values such as helping others, or condemning bullying, or caring for the environment were observed in the children's discussion of their relationships. In their book *Listening to children on the spiritual journey*, Stonehouse and May (2010) confirm that showing compassion is an important mark of spiritual growth. It was not clear in my research, which came first, the relationships or the values, but the two phenomena possibly developed simultaneously.

Reaching for transcendence in the natural world

The children at the rural school were very uncomfortable with Big Questions. They preferred to talk about their pets, or problems on the farm. Mitchell was an example of this discomfort with speculation. He avoided discussion about the beginning of the world and God, and about death. During these discussions he looked nervous, fiddling with his fingers. The researcher commented to the group, "I don't think kids at (this school) are into wondering". They all nodded. The group agreed that most of their community was concerned about surviving the drought, how to "get by". Mitchell expressed their concerns as "making sure you've got feed for your animals". Within his own environment, Mitchell was reaching beyond himself to the needs of their livestock.

Some children at the rural school did demonstrate a spiritual consciousness in "reaching beyond themselves". Kane chose for his "awesome" picture The Twelve Apostles, a group of off-shore rocks on the south-west coast of Victoria. He liked the ocean in the picture, that it was "all shiny", and he liked the different shapes of the rocks, and that it was a place with which he was familiar. He also liked being immersed in the cool water of the ocean on a hot day. He volunteered that he admired the eagles in his neighbourhood. He liked watching them fly so high, and then swoop on their prey. Kane's beautiful self-portrait seemed to illustrate his sense of a world transcending his present one. His self-portrait was drawn quickly, small, and in the centre of the page. Then, during the further discussion he filled the upper part of the page with clouds and sky-scrapers, the latter with scores of coloured windows. In the lower part of the picture he drew a path leading the figure to the sky-scrapers. He later confided that his ambition was to be "a house designer".

Luke also found transcendent experience in the ocean. He has been a skilled surfer since he was able to stand up on a boogie board at the age of three. Currently he used a full sized board. I asked him what he thought about when he's out in the surf. He said, "It looks good when they (other surfers) are inside a wave". When asked how he felt when he is inside a wave, he replied "It's like paradise". When I asked for clarification he agreed that he felt like he was in another world, where time stopped.

Kane and Luke were not very verbally fluent, but both expressed their spirituality through the *sensitive mode*. Kane was able to enter imaginatively into the visual world of the picture of The Twelve

Apostles. He sensed visually the shapes of the rocks and the shiny water as he had seen them when he had been present. He was able to recreate through memory the tactile sensation of cool ocean water. During the interview he also created fantastic shapes with the interlocking felt pens while he was talking. With his visual imagination he created images of beauty, charged with joy, which may symbolise transcendence. These images included the height of the eagle's flight, and the height, and mass of his sky scrapers. This picture had other features which may be symbols of the transcendent, such as the many coloured windows, as though they were inviting the viewer to enter a transcendent space. The figure of Kane on the path to the skyscrapers was redolent of a symbolic journey. Kane did not verbally explain this journey as any more than his desire to be a "house designer", but the drawing spoke of something more, a spiritual journey to a "celestial city".

Luke's experience of being inside the wave appeared to be a similar journey through sensory experience to something transcendent. Luke seemed to be "in paradise" because he achieved what could be described as a spiritual unity or connectedness between his action and experience. An interpretation of Luke's experience may be found in Rudolph Otto's (1923/1958) concept of the "numinous", a term he coined to describe transcendent experiences. Otto described two types of numinous experience: *mysterium tremendum* which is "wholly other", and *fascinans* which is an experience of "something more" (Merkur, 2006, p. 207-208). Luke's experience in the surf, which he described as being in "paradise", was for him something more than just being inside a wave. He reported that it had a timeless quality which he did not seek. His experience did not invoke the dread associated with *mysterium tremendum*, but was the beautiful, joyous experience of *fascinans*. According to Otto "the living 'something more' of the *fascinans*, the element of fascination" (Otto, 1923/1958, p. 35) may be found in experiences of many different religions, (and presumably) outside of formal religion.

Tom, from the suburban school, also seemed to be trying to describe an experience of "something other" in this conversation:

> Tom: I wish my family had a mansion for a house.
>
> W: Oh, why do you wish that?
>
> Tom: Because it would be cool if we had a veranda and we lived right next to the sea. And we could look out on the waves....
>
> W: What do you like about the sea?
>
> Tom: I like it at night when the sun goes down, because that's what we did once. We got in our car. We went home and had tea and we came back, and then the sun was just about to go down (smile).
>
> W: Oh, you saw it over the water and it was lovely!
>
> Tom: And then we took a picture- but it's kind of blurry ...

In this extract Tom demonstrated the *sensitive mode*, in particular, the visual aspects of his spirituality, his pleasure at looking at the waves, and the special experience of seeing the sun set over the water. In other parts of his interview he demonstrated other sensory modes, such as the tactile sense of digging in the sand, or being "buried" in sand, and the kinaesthetic pleasure of trying to balance on a boogie board in the surf. For Tom, these experiences seemed to be moments of "an unusual level of consciousness or perceptiveness, relative to other passages of conversation spoken by that child" which Hay & Nye (2006, p. 109) defined as *Relational Consciousness*. The *relational mode* was demonstrated in his wanting to share with his family the experience of having a house by the sea. He related the shared experience of driving in the car together, having tea, and going back to the beach to see the sun go down, then trying to take a photograph of this special shared event. Tom's *existential mode* of spirituality was demonstrated in several ways. His experiences of time included wanting to experience some permanence of his enjoyment of the sea, in wishing to own a house on the foreshore. He was also aware of the passing of time, and the way an instant can be precious, in the family going back to the beach to see the moment of sunset. Taking a photograph would be a way of trying to give permanence to that moment. His experiences of the sea gave Tom a special sense of place, for himself and his family. Tom's narrating of the experience of the sunset demonstrated his sense of awe and wonder, perhaps a glimpse of a transcendent reality. Finally, his regret that the picture was blurry, may show that he was aware that human experience is imperfect and impermanent.

Tom's experiences of the natural beauty of the sea and the sunset did not appear to be interpreted by him as "spiritual" in that he made no connection with God or any sense of the transcendent, but he did seem to have a sense of connectedness with nature and with his shared experience with his family. Tom's experiences may be a "natural precursor" to a deeper spiritual awakening. As Crawford and Rossiter (2006) wrote:

> Youth spirituality also includes response to the natural environment and beautiful things as well as personal concerns like fulfilment, happiness and community; if not a part of youth spirituality, these can at least be regarded as natural precursors or pathways to spirituality – avenues to the spiritual to which young people are attuned, or areas to which spirituality can be applied (p. 204)

Other writers may interpret Tom's experience as essentially spiritual. Ó Murchú (1997) maintained that spirituality is a natural human disposition. Hart (2003) maintained that we should consider ourselves as spiritual beings who have human experiences. Champagne (2003) based her belief that she saw small children expressing spirituality on the theology of the Incarnation (God the Son coming to earth as a human being). She believed that in a similar way to Christ uniting God's spirit and human flesh in himself, in human spirituality one is "incorporated in the world and not disconnected from it" (p. 46).

Tom's experience of the sea and the sunset appeared to be more than awe and wonder at external perceptions and events, and to be part of his *being in himself*. The researcher's overall impression of Tom was that externally he was tough, (the vice-principal reported that he was even violent to his little sister on occasions), very athletic, and not inclined to empathise with other people, but he longed to commune with nature. This latter trait was exhibited in his Journey drawing of himself alone on an island, where he could "do what (he wanted) for once". However, as Crawford and Rossiter (2006) pointed out, this longing is just a beginning of spirituality, and needs to be nurtured and developed more fully. Tom's *sensitive mode* of spirituality could be enriched by the development of his *relational mode*, and an encouragement to explore the transcendental mysteries of existence. This was demonstrated later in this chapter, in the incident with the sick bird where he did not seem to relate emotionally to the bird in the way that the other children did.

There were other instances of the children in the study "reaching beyond themselves" in a spiritual relationship with the earth, in particular with the Australian landscape. Sometimes this spiritual response was stimulated by one of the series of photographs shown to them in the first interview. A number of the children chose the picture of Uluru (formerly known as Ayer's Rock), because of its size and age, its iconic status for Australia and its history. For the children at the coastal school, where the rehearsal of the interviews was conducted, the landscape had significance beyond their own lives. Aimee said of Uluru, "I always wonder how it got there because it's so big, and you can see spear marks. Yes, you can tell it's got tracks all over it – ages ago aborigines have been there". Aimee related to the rock as having an ancient history which was significant to her as an Australian. Finn, from the suburban school, referred to Uluru as "an Australian icon". These children seemed to relate to this feature of the landscape as having spiritual significance for Australia's original inhabitants and for themselves. Aimee had a similar spiritual perspective about the aboriginal heritage of the coastline where she lived. Ryan, from the coastal school, wondered at the beauty of a picture of a pelican flying into the sunrise near his home. He translated this wonder into a concern to preserve the environment. He said, "I don't believe in God, but I hate what people are doing to his planet". At the provincial school, Caleb also related care of the environment with God's purpose. He said, "I reckon God probably made (Uluru) and made it in a certain spot, so the first people in Australia, the Australian aborigines could have it for themselves."

These children related to features of the earth through their *sensitive mode* in their awe and wonder at the immensity and colour of the rock, and the beauty of the pelican's flight. They bonded with the rock in the sense that they identified with it as part of their national heritage. They also exhibited bonding and empathy with the original inhabitants of Australia, as when Aimee saw physical evidence of their presence there, and was sensitive to their history and traditional claims to Uluru. Ryan and Caleb followed their *relational mode* a step further, into the existential and ethical domains. Out of their relationship with the earth they came to value its preservation. Although he said that he didn't believe in God, Ryan expressed regret at what humanity was doing to spoil the Creator's planet. He expressed a sense of moral obligation to care for the planet. Caleb had a sense that God had a purpose in creating the world, and particular places such as Uluru. He sensed that that purpose was the wellbeing of humanity, and perhaps Caleb had earth's other creatures in mind too.

Relating to animals

Children in each of the schools had a strong relationship to animals, especially their pets. At the suburban school this was particularly apparent. Hahn had a large number of animals at home, which she preferred to human company because "they don't talk". Pham's closest friend seemed to be her dog, which dominated both of her drawings and her conversation. The twins, Amanthi and Spencer, were especially fond of birds, and told stories of rescuing baby birds or eggs that had fallen out of the nest. In almost every group a girl chose the picture of the baby bird as awesome, and this generated discussion about caring for the environment. The following is a transcript of a conversation between Hanh, Finn, Pham and Tom at the suburban school. The children were discussing what they felt about the photograph of a newly hatched small bird, held in a man's hand; what they thought about little birds.

> Pham: I think they are really cute, because, and I actually held a bird at school once. It was a baby bird. I offered it a worm, but it wouldn't eat it.
>
> Finn: Also I was there with that bird. I think it had bird flu.
>
> W: I don't think so. It was sick, was it?
>
> Finn: It was really fluffed up (demonstrates with his hands, and crouching forward).
>
> Tom: Oh, that's when they're scared.
>
> Finn: It was fluffed up and it was going (makes gasping sniffs through his nose) sort of.
>
> W: Oh, it was really sick…it might have fallen out of the nest.
>
> (Finn has his fingers in his mouth, looking concerned).
>
> (Hahn has her back to the camera, and is watching the speakers).
>
> Pham: It couldn't actually fly. It was going (makes flapping motion with her hands) just flapping its wings and then it would just lie there.
>
> Finn: It just jumped instead of flying (demonstrates jumping movements).

W: Oh, poor little bird. So how did that make you feel when you saw that little bird that couldn't fly?

Pham: Um, it made me feel –

Finn: Sad.

Pham: Um.

Finn: Sorry for it.

Pham: It made me feel that I wanted to keep that bird.

W: And look after it?

(Pham nods).

Tom looks bored, not joining the conversation, yawns, and sits with hands on his head and his elbows on the table.

Finn: When we were at (another suburb) we were at this house, and there was this bird. And you could see its skeleton and all its skin was drying up (touched face, eyes are wide open).

Tom looks interested.

W: It was a skeleton?

Finn: No it was alive, and it was in the house.

W changes the topic of conversation.

This is an interesting episode because it contained a wealth of material on the *sensitive mode of being*. Although the children in the study were older than Champagne's (2003) pre-school children, and were more skilled at verbal communication, they sometimes responded with their whole body. Their responses to the memory of the sick bird were tactile (how it felt to hold the bird), visual and kinaesthetic (the fluffed up feathers and the ineffective efforts to fly). Finn, in particular, responded by imitating the bird's movements, and by facial expressions of his emotions. His verbal responses were both empathetic (he said he felt sad) and also intellectual, in that he tried to explain the condition as "bird flu". It was a holistic response. The children also demonstrated their *relational mode of being* in this incident.

Finn expressed his feeling for the bird. Pham wanted to care for the bird. She tried to feed it worms, and she wanted to take it home and look after it. Hahn seemed to be expressing her empathy with the bird by directing her attention to the speakers, although she said nothing. In various ways, these children were demonstrating empathy with the sick bird.

The children's response to the sick bird has parallels with Hyde's (2008) concept of *felt sense,* which Hyde described as follows:

> The felt sense, as a characteristic of children's spirituality identified in my study, entails the attending to physical bodily awareness on the part of the individual. Each child's corporeality seemed to act as a primal source of knowledge which enabled them to draw upon their own bodily wisdom as a means by which to get in touch with the felt sense in a particular situation (p. 88).

Hyde referred to this process as *focusing,* which involves attending to the bodily awareness of situations, persons, or events, as a way of getting in touch with the spiritual dimension of *the felt sense* (Hyde, 2008, p. 86). In the conversation given above, the children, particularly Finn and Pham, demonstrated their bodily identification with what was happening to the sick bird. In this identification they were also demonstrating bonding and empathy.

The demonstration of *existential mode* appeared in the children's attempt to explain why the bird was sick. Tom, who displayed very little emotional response, contributed intellectually to the discussion with "facts" about birds. Pham, on the other hand, tried to analyse her feelings about the bird, in considering her desire to care for it.

In the following extract Caleb showed a development of the quality of Relational Consciousness in that he saw caring for animals and for people as part of a divine purpose. His *relational mode of spirituality* seemed to demonstrate formation of values and a rationale for those values. He believed that it is good to care for animals because they are God's creation.

> Caleb said, "I reckon we should care for birds because God created them to make us respect all living creatures and animals. And we should also give lots of animals water to help them survive as well as us. With the birds, we can also take care of them, like, if they don't know where they are going ... like they might fly into a tree or get injured, we can take them to the vet."

When confronted with the question of who might be "in charge of the universe", Caleb's response was "I would say 'Hi', nice to meet you – but we are all in charge of the universe, and other people are living here in community too."

This section sought to demonstrate the children's spirituality in their empathy with animals, especially vulnerable ones. They demonstrated this bonding and empathy through their bodily responses and through trying to find intellectual explanations for animals' sufferings. Caleb expressed this concern in value terms, as a God-given responsibility to care for God's creatures.

Relating to other children

The sense of belonging to a human community informed the bonding, empathy and value formation of many of the children. Human relationships are more complex than relationships with the natural world. Therefore it was to be expected that *relational modes of spirituality* would be more complex. This was demonstrated in the extracts cited below. The children's peer relationships were marked by caring and a sense of justice. This was expressed most explicitly by some of the girls, and demonstrated by both boys and girls in physical action. Below are some extracts from the profiles of children at the provincial school, followed by transcripts from the suburban school, which are indicative of this feature.

Grace described her peer relationships as follows. She said "when Kerry's upset I help her, because I say 'what's wrong? Has anybody hurt your feelings?' And she talks to me. And I say to that person 'You should say sorry, and you shouldn't do that again'. If they don't listen to me I go to the teacher".

Billy described his friendships in terms of what they did together. He gave a list of the names of his friends, and told how they play football and "chasey" together, and dig in the sand pit.

Pham, at the suburban school, described a negative aspect of peer relationships:

> W: What are bad things people do?
>
> Pham (thinks); Well Rachel has been bossy to me. Like, before she liked me, now everything she says, we say OK with her. And now she thinks that we are so easy on her that she hasn't to do anything.
>
> W: Oh, so she takes advantage of you?
>
> Pham: Yes, when I almost tripped over on her she said "Why did you push me?"

Harry, at the suburban school, discussed the operation of friendship on the soccer field.

> Harry: During our soccer one of my team mates got hit by a ball on the back. And when I passed the ball to my friend I just stopped immediately, and then I started running at my friend, running after my friend, and I picked him up, and then I asked him how he was, yes, and then the coach came... (On another occasion) when I got kicked on the face, I fell down and stuff, and I cried. And then most of my team came, and then they put me on the sidelines to heal.

The children who took part in the study frequently described friendship in terms of helping a peer who was hurt. This was primarily a *sensitive* response to an event like a child falling down and crying. However other children, especially boys like Billy expressed friendship as what they did when playing together. However, these extracts gave more emphasis to the *relational mode of being*. Billy showed his bonding with his friends by naming them. The bonding of friendship occurred in these extracts in the playground, the classroom and the sports field. The children demonstrated empathy in that they responded emotionally to the hurt of their friends, and by running to help. When Harry described going to help his friend on the soccer field there was a breathlessness and urgency in his language. When Grace helped her friend, she expressed her sympathy to the victim, and outrage to the bully. Pham's language, when relating the loss of a friendship, expressed her pain and confusion. There was a complexity of value formation expressed in these extracts. Most of the children implied that they valued loyalty, and care for their friends' physical and emotional needs. They agreed that bullying was wrong and needed to be addressed by shaming the bully or appealing to a person in authority. Wrongdoers should repent and apologise. They believed that they had a right to appeal to someone in authority to administer justice. Looking at the *existential mode* suggests that these are some universals of human experience which the children were experiencing. Friendship is a rewarding two-way experience, and loss of friendship can be painful. Pain and hurt are universal human experiences. In addition, we live in an orderly society where we expect there is someone in charge to maintain order and administer justice.

In reaching out to their peers these children seemed to demonstrate their spirituality as a sense of connectedness with the Other in their shared actions, and feelings for their peers. de Souza (2003) referred to this aspect of spirituality as "the human person's movement towards Ultimate Unity" (p. 276). In some cases this may be manifest as *integrating awareness* (Hyde, 2008). For example, when Harry was playing soccer, he was concentrating on passing the ball, and was simultaneously aware that his friend was hurt and prepared to go to his aid. For Hyde, this ability to "integrate an emerging wave of consciousness with a previous level" constituted a characteristic of spirituality (p. 105).

The children in this research demonstrated their spirituality in their bonding and empathy through caring for other children, especially when physically hurt, or bullied. Even in the midst of a game, they were aware of the needs of others. In this they demonstrated the values of caring for others, and loyalty to friends. They also valued justice for their friends, and the need for adults to be in charge. Friendships also introduced them to the existential mysteries of love and loss.

Relating to families

This topic was introduced after the reading of *The Violin Man*, where the main character had no family except his daughter who had died. The groups were asked "What's good about having a family? What's not so good about having a family?" Relationships with family members were commonly expressed in terms of what families do. Mitchell, at the rural school, gave a fairly typical response to the idea of being without a family.

> I'd feel sad and lonely and bored…You get to play with them. They can buy you stuff. (Families) could drive you somewhere, like to a playground or somewhere. Or when you play sport they can drive you to it.

Alex, from the provincial school, had given the value of his family more thought. Below are extracts from his profile.

> Oscar (in The Violin Man) would be pretty lonely, but he still had his friends. It's good (having friends) because if you were by yourself, like if everyone was died and you were 10 years old, and you were grown up by yourself, you'd have to

ride to school and everything, get a job, somehow buy all your food and everything…

Having a family (is special), you've got people to look after you. They can help you, talk to you sometimes. (I can ask my mum) stuff about her cancer, and only she's sick. A sad thing, we have to look after her. She can't do many things, can't walk for 400 metres…(I have to) help her, take the bins out, riding home, let her sleep, have to let her have a rest.

Alex also told how he was proud of his sister for being a district athletics champion. He also has a great affection for his two nanas, one of whom bakes him cakes and makes him feel special. He wants to mow her lawn for her when he is bigger. Alex has learned to reach beyond himself in his family relationships.

Finn had some negative as well as positive experiences of family. Below are some extracts and summaries from his profile.

"Everything is good about your family. Your mum and dad help you get breakfast. Your brother and sister can play with you. And your mum and dad can buy you toys and things. Well, it would be hard for you to do anything – and you'd have to live on the streets." What is not good about having a family is "when your mum and dad split up, or divorce"…

Finn's parents were divorced, and his father lived in another state. He seemed to have his strongest relationship with his father, whom he often quoted to the other children during group activities. A highlight of Finn's life was when his father took him and his sister on a holiday to Malaysia. Finn used many gestures and an excited voice while he told a story about being chased by dangerous monkeys. He said "I went 'Dad! Dad! Dad! He picked me up. He looked at where the monkey (was) and then, and he picked me up and we ran all the way to the hotel". During the interviews Finn expressed a preoccupation with danger and violence, and he seemed to be very angry about his father leaving. At the end of the final interview I asked him "Do you miss your Dad?" He gave an uncharacteristically quiet response "Yes, I miss him very much."

Because children are so completely dependent on families for their material and emotional needs, it was predictable that children such as Mitchell, Alex and Finn should first express their relationship to their families through their *sensitive mode of being,* through tangible benefits like food and shelter, and someone to drive them to the football. In the case of Alex, this need for material security was most poignantly expressed, as he was facing the possibility of his mother's death. However, the children's main focus, whatever mode they used, was on their primary social relationship, their bonding with their family. Champagne (2003) spoke of the process of *filiation* by which young children internalise their relationship with their parents or the benevolent adults who care for them. For young children, adults provide the order which allows a child to construct their inner self (p. 47). Hyde (2008) made a similar observation when he said that families provide a sense of identity for children; and "a Collective Self in which the relationship of each to Other was inseparable in defining each other's being" (pp. 131-132).

Mary, from the provincial school, expressed this sense of identity as "I'm a special person, because I have a mum and a dad, and some people don't." For Mary, having an intact and stable family made her feel uniquely loved, and it also made her aware of her less fortunate friends. Alex observed, when considering Oscar in *The Violin Man*, that friends are valuable for support, but they are not an adequate substitute for a family. He noted the mutual support that he and his mother gave each other, and the mutual support within his wider family, including his grandmothers and his sister. Through these relationships Alex was learning the value of mutual care for the needs of each family member, and forming his identity within the circle of the family. Existentially, Alex was becoming aware that he was not alone, but part of a web of mutual love. Finn, like Alex, had to cope with loss in his family. On the one hand Finn spoke of a harmonious family, eating and playing together, but he also had to cope with the reality of the parents' divorce and his father's absence. The family split meant he had to reassess his identity as a family member (Hyde, 2008, p.131). He seemed to be compensating for his father's absence through his violent imaginative life, and by constantly referring to his father in conversation. His repetition of the phrase "he picked me up" seemed to be a poignant expression of his continuing bond with his father. That Finn empathises with other families who have lost their security, in particular, the loss of a father or a son, was reflected in his reaction to the picture of refugees. He said "They're feeling sad because their son might get hurt, or their husband or something."

Through their relationships with their families these children were learning about the mutuality of family love and protection, and a sense of their own identity. They expressed their awareness of this relationship through their *sensitive* as well as their *relational mode*. As with their friends, but in a more intense way, they were experiencing, in their *existential mode*, how to cope with love and loss.

Summary: Reaching out through relationships

Reflection on the children's relationship with the natural world, other people, and indirectly on themselves has given an overview of the way Champagne's (2003) *spiritual modes of being* can give an insight into the way the children's relationships formed their spirituality. It demonstrated the way they bonded with significant others, how they demonstrated empathy with the situations and feelings of others, and the way their relationships informed their moral values. In the ordinary events of their relationships the children demonstrated at times a "new dimension of understanding, meaning, and experience

... a special sense that added value to their ordinary or everyday perspective" (Hay & Nye, 2006, p. 109). They were demonstrating what Hay and Nye called "relational consciousness".

Conclusion

This chapter presented an overview of the children in the study "reaching beyond themselves". This was expressed in their sense of wonder and awe about the natural world, and existential issues of beginnings and of death and the transcendent. It was also expressed in their relationships with the natural world and with other people. Through the lens of Champagne's (2003) *spiritual modes of being* this chapter examined the children's spirituality, their connecting with the world beyond themselves through their senses, their relationships and their reflection on existential mysteries. The children's curiosity was directed to how the natural world worked, in a scientific sense, and as a reflection of some higher purpose. Although most of these children were not overtly religious they were curious about the possibility of a transcendent realm of God and heaven, and of a purpose in creation and human life. They were also sensitive to the transcendent qualities of the natural world. In their relationships with the natural world, and their friends and families, the children valued caring, protection and justice, and were learning to address the degradation of nature, and the imperfections as well as the joys of human relations.

Practical applications for teaching religious education

There are topics which are commonly sources of awe and wonder for children: the world of nature, including its origin and purpose, and the beginning and end of human life. These topics are points of contact for exploring children's concerns about meaning, and the presence of God.

Children's mutual relationships with nature, animals, other children, and families are very important to them. They should be encouraged for their own sakes, and as an insight into the possibility of developing a personal relationship of mutuality, trust and love with God.

Out of their various relationships children develop their system of values, an understanding of right and wrong, and a sense of their own worth and identity. This can help them relate to Christian values, and a sense of their worth to God.

The work of Champagne, Hyde, and other researchers, as well as the observations of this research, also suggest some practical methods for the classroom.

Children can be encouraged to explore the lesson through the application of Champagne's *spiritual modes of being*. Opportunity should be given for children to use their senses: visual, auditory, tactile, and kinaesthetic, to engage with a Biblical story or lesson.

They can learn through relationships, through interaction with others in the class, or by drawing on their life experiences of family, friends, or the natural world.

These experiences can lead them to existential questions about values, and deeper meanings they derive from their engagement with the lesson.

References

Champagne, E. (2003). Being a child: A spiritual child. *International Journal of Children's Spirituality.* 8 (1), 43-53.

Crawford, M & Rossiter, G. (2006). *Reasons for Living: Education and Young People's Search for Meaning, Identity and Spirituality.* Melbourne: ACER.

de Souza. M. (2003). Contemporary influences on the spirituality of young people: Implications for education. *International Journal of Children's Spirituality,* 8 (3), 269-279.

Hart, T. (2003). *The Secret Spiritual World of Children.* Makawao, HI: Inner Ocean.

Hay, D. (2000). Spirituality versus individualism: Why we should nurture relational consciousness. *International Journal of Children's Spirituality,* 5 (1), 37-48.

Hay, D & Nye, R. (2006). *The Spirit of the Child.* (Rev. ed.). London: Jessica Kingsley.

Horell, H. (2003). Cultural postmodernity and Christian faith formation. In T. Groome & H. Horell (Eds.). *Horizons and Hopes: The Future of Religious Education,* (pp. 81-105). New York, NY: Paulist Press.

Hyde, B. (2008). *Children and Spirituality: Searching for Meaning and Connectedness.* London: Jessica Kingsley.

Merkur, D. (2006). Interpreting numinous experience. *Social Analysis,* 50 (2). 204-223.

ó Murchú, D. (1997). *Reclaiming Spirituality: A New Spiritual Framework for Today's World.* Dublin: Gill & Macmillan.

Otto, R. (1923/1958). *The Idea of the Holy.* (J. Narvey Trans.). London: Oxford University Press.

Stonehouse, C. & May, S. (2010). *Listening to Children on the Spiritual Journey: Guidance for Those who Teach and Nurture.* Grand Rapids, MI: Baker Academic.

Thompson, C. (2004). *The Violin Man.* Sydney: Hodder Children's Books.

Wright, A. (2000). *Spirituality and Education.* London: Routledge/Falmer.

4

Reaching within Themselves:
Consciousness and relationality (2)

Introduction

"Spirituality has been described in contemporary literature as a level of connectedness that a person may feel towards themselves, their communities, the world around them and to a 'Transcendent Other'" (de Souza 2003, p. 271). The previous chapter discussed the children's capacity to "reach beyond themselves" in awe and wonder. This was manifested in their relationships with the transcendent, the natural world and other people. This chapter looks particularly at findings relating to children's connectedness with themselves, and their reaching within for spiritual strength. It goes on to examine the ways in which the children's communities help them develop moral values and a sense of direction in their lives. Ultimately, children try to make sense of their lives through developing an individual "story" of who they are: their individual identity.

De Souza (2003) pointed out that resilience and a sense of connectedness are important for mental, physical, social and emotional well-being, which ought to be provided by family and community structures, for the nurture of the inner life. She described this inner spiritual life as a movement towards Ultimate Unity, "an ever-swirling spiral built with layers of accumulated learning and experiences which span a lifetime" (p. 276). Some of the children in this study demonstrated an interaction or stream between their experiences of the outer world and their inner reflection which, even in their short lives, seemed to fit this spiral model. de Souza, and Hyde (2007), have reviewed the body of research which indicated that to address the inner as well as the outer lives of students in religious education programs, time must be given to engaging the senses, thoughts, feelings, intuition and imagination.

This chapter gives some insights into the ways in which the children in the study used their feelings, intuition and imagination to develop their inner lives. Hay and Nye (2006) observed that children have strategies to maintain their sense of the spiritual, to preserve their inner life from assaults from a world that is sometimes hostile to their spiritual dimension. These strategies included "efforts to mentally and physically withdraw from mundane distractions, attempts to consciously focus or concentrate on a particular subject, seeking relation or communication through prayer, seeking and exploiting aesthetic and sensory experiences, and deliberately 'philosophising'" (p. 123).

This chapter particularly examines findings relating to children's connectedness with themselves, and their reaching within for spiritual strength. The findings in this study are consistent with many of Coles' (1990) observation about children who have faced all kinds of adversity. Some examples were Margarita from Brazil (p. 95) whose Christian faith supported her in a life of poverty, and Natalie the Hopi child whose inner life was in harmony with her physical environment (p. 152). Ginny, living in difficult family circumstances, described herself as "marching through life" (p. 322), and Eric used his mental resources to deal with difficult inner questioning (p. 283). All of those children demonstrated resilience through being able to reach within themselves. Some of the sources of this inner strength which children use include prayer (Mountain, 2005), and development of the imagination (Mountain, 2007). Ken Wilbur (2001) described the way in which children can incorporate new experiences into a higher level of awareness, or a more integrated Self. Examples in this research seemed to demonstrate that the children internalised experiences from their lives in the world to produce a deeper level of resilience and inner strength, a more integrated Self.

Meditation and Self discipline

The following example of "reaching within themselves" was taken from a variety of observations and texts of the interviews with Harry. Harry, at the suburban school, was looking for strength to face tension and anxiety. When I first met him he was walking along, stretching his arms. In his self-portrait his arms are stretched out. He explained that he liked to stretch the muscles in his arms and neck when they became tense and they hurt. He variously explained this tension as due to running about too much at school, or "after a hard day's work at school". When I asked him did he worry a lot, he said "only when I might get hurt". Later he said he worried about "around the world, like anything happens, like any type of sickness, or anything that would happen. You worry about it, like if there's a bomb (in Iraq or London at the time)". Harry said he could go to his mother when he was worried, and "she makes good meals and that". Harry also went to the park to think. For his Journey picture he drew the trees and the grass at the park. Then he drew himself sitting under the tree reading a book. He said that his grandmother sat nearby and waited for him. He said, "Sometimes I lie down and look at the birds and the sky. Then the wind just blows on me, and cools me down, after a hard day at school." He told me he thought about waterfalls, water in a lake, or about the ocean and fishes. He also thought about "me and my dad kicking a ball around the park. Those are the things that make me happy". Or, where he finds his strength. He said that he is Buddhist, but doesn't think about it much, but "when I grow up I will." For Harry religion is something that old people like his grandmother practise. But now, as a child, he seemed to be practising meditation and self discipline in a Buddhist way. I said "But still when you need to be strong, you think your own thoughts?" "Yes" he said.

Harry was demonstrating an interaction between his outer environment and his inner life. He was using his *sensitive mode* to connect with the sensations of tension in his limbs, or his visual and tactile sensations when he sat in the park and connected with the cool breeze, the trees and the birds. In his imagination he related with waterfalls and lakes which were not actually present. He used his *relational* mode to integrate his consciousness of his grandmother sitting nearby, or memories of playing football with his father, into a new awareness. His religion seemed to provide a source of inner strength for him, at least through his grandmother's practice. More importantly, he practised a form of meditation in the park, and of self discipline for his body at school. This was consistent with following some aspects of the Buddhist Noble Eightfold Path (Snelling, 1992). Harry seemed to be carrying out spiritual exercises consistent with Right Thought (switching from selfish thoughts to more altruistic ones), Right Effort (being "aware and awake in each moment…to make each activity of (the) day meditation" (1992, p. 61), and Right Mindfulness and Concentration (not in full-scale meditation, but in quiet and directed contemplation).

Resilience

Grace, at the provincial school, was another child who demonstrated inner spiritual strength. These extracts are from her profile.

> Death and illness loomed large in her family. She said in one interview that all her uncles had asthma. One uncle died a month previously and she was grieving for him. When the other children were discussing death she folded her arms and looked away. Grace believed that God was really

important, because he made us, but she did not make an overt connection between God and her everyday life. Grace agreed that her health has been a dominating issue in her life. The only wish she expressed was to have no eczema or asthma.

I asked her what she did when she felt sad. She said "I go to a quiet place…I just sit down and think". When she was happy she would go to the playground and play with her friends.

Grace's Journey picture was of herself sitting at a desk, writing stories. She would like to have a room of her own where she could write. This was a shy confession, accompanied by much scratching and wriggling, and nodding to my prompting questions. I got the impression that she felt that her experiences had given her stories to tell, and she said she wanted her books to make people happy.

Grace demonstrated considerable fortitude and positive attitude in dealing with her life's disadvantages, such as chronic ill health, the disfigurement of her eczema, and her physical and intellectual limitations. She was not able to articulate to any degree what the sources of her inner strength were, but there were some clues in the text. She seemed to have considerable support from significant people in her life. Her family was with her when she was sick and in hospital. She made positive comments about her family, such as saying that her father was her hero, and that he was a chef who made delicious meals. Her friends at school were considerate of her needs and offered support. This was observed by the researcher as well as reported by Grace. At the first interview Mary sat beside her, used encouraging words, and put her arm around her when Grace appeared uncomfortable in the strange situation. She mentioned two special friends, Kerry, who had been in the same class since Prep, and another friend who had known her "since I was born". The mutual support between Grace and Kerry was mentioned in the previous chapter. This empathy with other people in distress was demonstrated in her reaction to the picture of the refugees. In her profile it was noted that "her face expressed real distress that they were escaping from a war". She said 'It's not nice to have wars … We should stop the fighting so they can go back'" Grace had a specific strategy for dealing with negative emotions. She said "I go to a quiet place…I just sit down and I think". Her strategy seemed to be an exercise in "time out", which is encouraged at the school. For example, Billy reported that he took "time out" when he felt angry. The source of Grace's inner strength, her spiritual strength was largely a mystery. [5]

Literature on resilience can assist one to understand Grace's inner strength. Medical research makes a link between resilience and family support in children with chronic asthma (Frieze, 2008). A review of psychological research into resilience (Wright & Masten, 2005) defined resilience as "a pattern of positive adaptation in the context of past or present adversity" (p. 18). Examples of assets and protective factors which contribute to resilience include child, family, community, and cultural characteristics (p. 24).

Grace had a positive outlook on life, and (possibly) faith and a sense of meaning in life. She did not seem to have the advantage of good cognitive abilities and problem-solving skills. However Grace seemed to have the advantage of family characteristics, including a stable and supportive home environment, and parents who were involved in her education and welfare. Grace indicated that she perceived that she was well supported in developing a positive outlook on life. These are characteristics which indirectly indicate Grace's spirituality, for which concepts like *relational consciousness* (Hay & Nye, 2006) or *spiritual modes of being* (Champagne, 2003) are clearer indicators.

---

5 I met Grace, at the dentist, in 2009. The change was amazing. Her skin was clear, she had put on weight, and she appeared healthy and confident. Her father, who was with her, said that she had largely overcome her health problems.

Sport and physical activity

For most of the children who took part in the study, physical activity and sport were sources of wonder and delight for their own sakes, and an immediate way of expressing themselves non-verbally. They were also inner resources through which they explored their spiritual potential, and a way of connecting with the earth and other people. Engebretson's (2007) study of the spirituality of teenage boys recorded older boys' sense of joy experienced through sport and physical achievement. She recorded the following examples:

> Playing football and running. Very basic emotions are used when playing football. There's nothing to worry or think about just the game and the ball ...
>
> The first wave I ever caught while surfing. I dropped into the inside of the wave and was surfing in the inside of the tube. Being surrounded by all that water was the only time I had ever felt fully alive (Engebretson, 2007, p. 17).

Cooper (1998) recorded the following statement:

> Sport cannot equal the sacred traditions as a means of cultivating the inner life. But ... sport does possess its own unique genius for revealing and opening to people the spirit's 'gem-like flame' ... in its ability to provoke wonder, to elicit deep feeling, to grace our lives with glimpses of timeless beauty and freedom – in these and other ways sport, though not a religion, (is) something religious (Cooper, 1998, p.1).

In Cooper's *Playing in the Zone* (1998), he explored the phenomenon of heightened awareness, and the difficulty in communicating that experience, which elite athletes describe as being in the "zone". Some sports researchers use Maslow's term "peak experience", to describe being in the "zone". In my study, Luke, at the rural school, seemed to experience the spontaneous and transcendent quality of "peak experience", when he spoke of being in "paradise" while surfing. But experience of being in the "zone" seemed to occur for other children while playing sport. Harry's experience of kicking his second ball in the middle and scoring a goal (see extract below), was one of wonder and delight. David, at the coastal school, seemed to experience time standing still, when he would practise kicking a football in the back yard for long periods. Alex's rigorous training (see below) could prepare him for the "zone", when he achieved a "personal best".

Here are two extracts from the transcripts of Lucy and Harry, at the suburban school, discussing their feelings about sport.

> Lucy: I like sport, especially skipping … I'm not really a football type of person.
>
> (W: Is that because it's too rough?) Yes. And I don't like basketball because I get a bit scared of the ball if it hits me. So I don't like that either. And I think basketball is for tall people and I'm really short….I like (skipping) because I can do it by myself. I can do it really, really fast. And then if I do it with other people I can sing rhymes with it.
>
> Lucy also likes long jump, roller skating and riding her scooter.
>
> Harry: I'm a sporty person … I like soccer. I've got a club, like a team. And sometimes I play footy (Australian Rules football), because I can remember Auskick came to our school. And it was on the oval. And I played one match against my class. At first ball I almost scored, but it spun the wrong way and went out of bounds. And the second shot I got it in the middle. (W: And you got a goal?) Yes.

Both Lucy and Harry are of Asian origin, and for these children sport not only provides a personal challenge and enjoyment, but also is a way of making friends and establishing their identity as Australians, in a culture where sport has such a high priority. These extracts also demonstrated Champagne's (2003) *modes of being*. The *sensitive mode* was employed in their physical participation and enjoyment. They engaged their *relational mode* through teamwork and interpersonal action. Their *existential mode* seemed to be operational in that they achieved a sense of identity as good sportspersons and good Australians.

For children whose families have been in Australia for a long time sport can also be a primary way of expressing their joy and wonder. For Alex, at the provincial school, sport and physical activity played several roles. He enjoyed the pleasure of his bodily sensations. He found in sport an avenue for expressing his inner strength, his resolve and his identity. Sport also provided a focus for his relationship with his family and his friends. Here are some extracts from Alex's transcripts.

> Alex: (I picked the pole vaulter because) first, she's an Australian, and I like her… Pole vaulting is good to watch … I do athletics, and in seniors you can do pole vaulting. We do all sorts of events. Another new thing we do at athletics is hammer throw. It's like shot put, only you spin around and throw. (Alex demonstrates.) (Sport is also amazing) because you meet new friends, you learn things. And because I play soccer and football I might play AFL or World Cup, or I might be in the Commonwealth Games or the Olympics.

This is from a later conversation.

> W: When are you smiley?
>
> Alex: … When I win an award.
>
> W: What have you won awards for?
>
> Alex: Athletics. Last year I got the most PBs (Personal Bests) …. You do an event and then you do it again. You have a program. Say you did the 800 metres, and I did it again and I beat my time I'd get a PB. And so far (this year) I think I've got 4 PBs, and I've only been going 5 weeks. This is my fifth season … (My sister) Amy's been going for a long time so I thought I'd be doing it. And she's in under 13s this season.

Sport and physical activity seemed to do more than exercise Champagne's different modes of being. Sport seemed to be a vehicle through which these children integrated their activity in the outer physical world with their inner spiritual lives. It provided a way of "being-in-the-world" (Heidegger, 1980). That is, it provided an understanding of the truth about "who am I?" rather than just "what am I?" and how one relates to oneself and others. Through his sporting efforts Alex came to a deeper understanding of who he was and how he was valued by himself and his sporting and family communities. Alex's spirituality, or his "being-in-the-world", appeared to be demonstrated in his choice to integrate his culture's positive values of personal effort, physical achievement and social solidarity, into his self-image as a competent and valuable individual.

In physical activity and sporting achievement children are given the opportunity to reach within themselves. These activities seemed to enhance the spirituality of these children through their sensory awareness of their bodies and their physical and social environments, by developing their ability to relate to their team and their families, and by giving them insight into their individual meaning and worth as "beings in the world".

Imagination

Imagination was another means by which the children sought spiritual strength within themselves. Imagination, play, intuition are all means by which children engage with spirituality and communicate their spiritual insights and experiences. Champagne (2003) listed imagination as one of the keys to young children's *existential modes of being*. She wrote that "within time and space, within the existential quest of knowing through games, imitation, symbolism or imagination, lies the unfolding of the child's existence, of his/her *being-in-the-world*" (2003, p. 51). de Souza (2005) emphasised the importance of allowing children and young people to use their intuitive abilities as part of a learning process which integrates the whole person, mind, heart and soul. For Berryman (1991), "godly play" gives young children room and permission to explore existential questions, and get to know God through their imaginative activities (p.137). According to Hay and Nye (2006) the languages of fiction and play are significant ways in which children "framed their spirituality". Playfulness allowed a personalised and internal response to a story or situation, provided flexibility to play with an idea, and used language which was natural to the child rather than an alien religious expression (pp. 120-121). The texts below also demonstrate the children's use of imagination in developing empathy with other people, and moral values, which are markers of authentic spiritual qualities of "being-in-the-world-with-others" (Webster 2004). The children who took part in the research exercised their imagination in a number of these ways to explore and articulate their spirituality.

Sometimes imagination is just a fresh, playful way of perceiving the world. When Lizzy, at the rural school, chose a picture of two rocks standing off the shore she saw in it two pirate ships, and a small cloud between the "ships" became a puff of smoke from their guns as they fired at each other.

Some of the children at the rural school seemed to compensate for lack of first hand experience of the wider world with a rich imaginative life. For example, Bailey was a shy child whose everyday experiences seemed rather limited, but he had a rich imaginative life, which seemed to be fed by television and video games. He enjoyed sport, but was not in a local team, and did not seem to have travelled far from his small community. (Poverty seemed to be a family issue). Although he did not enjoy writing lessons, he told the researcher this story which he wrote in class, with a lot of prompting.

"I wrote this story about two kids. Their names were Kenny

and Carl. They were trying to run away from school. They managed to get away and there was this place called Coinland. And there was this petrol station, and they sell hovercars. And then they stole them. They raced along Coinland until they came to another land. And the police were after them … They just had normal cars. (W: And did they catch them?) No, they didn't get them. They got away."

Bailey told a number of other stories, from television shows. His most touching story was of what happened on the television series, "Meerkat Manor", which the rural children really enjoyed. He told how this meerkat "got bitten by a puff adder, and the venom did something to him. And his flesh was rotting away. And he survived". I asked did that make him a hero. Bailey replied, "Yes, courageous".

Ruth, at the provincial school, also had a rich imaginative life, and much of her relational experience was fed by books, films and the computer. She was able to draw on this experience to make sense of the world, as well as using her life experience to relate to characters in fiction. She observed that Oscar (in *The Violin Man*) was a little sad when he was alone, but happier when he was with other people. She related a story from a book about a girl who lived an imaginative life in a tree, then Ruth wondered if Oscar had an imaginary friend. "Maybe when he was lonely he had an imaginary friend … but when he had people he didn't need them." Ruth also related a movie story about a disabled boy, which is quoted below.

> I reckon they came deliberately (i.e. dinosaurs were created by God for a purpose even if they were going to die out) because I watched this movie and it was based on a true story. It was about this boy and he had really, really short legs and he couldn't walk properly. And his parents didn't care much about him. One time they were on a bus on the way to school and they came off somewhere and they went into the water. The boy always thought that God had a special

purpose for him, that he was meant to be like that because it was something special. And in the end he ended up saving someone's life that he got out of the water, but in the end he died.

Imagination, stimulated by literature and the popular media, enabled Bailey to explore the possibilities of life beyond the restrictions of his environment, and this exploration seemed to be shaping his values. From the story of the meerkats Bailey seemed to develop empathy with the suffering of others, and the value of courage in the face of suffering. More problematically, he seemed to accept that it was permissible to steal if you can get away with it (as often seems to happen in television drama). Ruth seems to have learned to empathise with real people through her identification with fictional characters. Through a movie she explored existential questions such as possible meanings in suffering, disability and rejection, and of God having a special purpose in people's lives. Through imaginative responses to the media Bailey and Ruth were reaching into themselves to explore new meanings. They exercised their *existential modes of being* to integrate outer experiences into their inner lives.

Not all of the children who were interviewed had a healthy spiritual life emanating from their imagination. Finn's imaginative world was full of violence, and disconnectedness. His favourite game which he played with his sister was *Lord of the Rings*, where he preferred to act as Gimli. "He's the guard with the battle-axe", he explained. He told long and graphic stories, with many gestures and a happy, excited voice, stories of himself in video games, shooting and killing. Finn's self portrait was a small figure of himself in the centre of the picture with a gun in each hand. He was surrounded by a sea of blood, in which was a dead "army man" ("not a kid"), and at the edge was a large bomb and a ring of cactuses. Finn presented as an angry little boy. He said, "When I'm angry I start to get smaller. So people can beat me easier … and I'm angry when I'm small". However, his aggression seemed to the researcher to be confined to his fantasy life. He loved war games because he "usually loves gory stuff", but he said he would not shoot a real person "unless I'm in a war". I did not observe any aggressive behaviour toward other children, and he declared that killing or hurting real people is wrong. He showed genuine concern for the plight of the refugees. He said, "They're feeling sad because their son might get hurt, or their husband or something". His three wishes were that there would be no such thing as war, that "everyone would never hurt anyone", and no-one would say bad words. Finn had another escape route in his imaginary world, which he described as crossing the Milky Way to another universe. It is possible that Finn was trying to work through his anger about being separated from his father (he talked a lot about his father), seeking to resolve it in his separate fantasy life.

In spite of his preoccupation with violent fantasies, Finn seemed to be drawing on the inner resources of his considerable intelligence and his imagination for spiritual strength. He seemed to be exploring violence as an interpersonal value and beginning to reject it. He seemed to be exploring the question "Am I a violent person?" And how to deal with his anger, when he said "When I'm angry I get smaller". The hurt in his family life seemed to enable him to empathise with other families, such as the refugees, who had suffered loss in their families. Finn seemed to be working to achieve integration in his life through his imagination. Hence he seemed to be achieving spiritual growth.

Symbols

Symbols, like imagination, play, and intuition, can be existential modes of expression of children's spirituality (Champagne, 2003, Moriarty, 2008). According to Carl Jung, a symbol is an object "that possesses specific connotations in addition to its conventional and obvious meaning ... It has a wider 'unconscious' aspect that is never precisely defined or fully explained" (Jung, 1964, p. 20, 21). For Jung, the function of symbols in the personal sphere is to aid growth by providing personal meaning. This occurs in the process of the development of the Self when excess psychic energy is unconsciously transformed into symbolic expressions, some of which appear to be universal to humanity and are termed "archetypes" (Jung, 1960/2001). Examination of the symbols in one's dreams, stories or art can not only lead to greater self-knowledge and development of personal unity, but can also give a person "knowledge of one's commonality, the universality of experience, and the creation of meaning from this experience" (Salman, 1997, p. 57). Paul Ricoeur, a French philosopher, valued symbols for their "surplus meaning". In *The Symbolism of Evil* (1967) he described three dimensions present in any authentic symbol – cosmic, oneiric (in dreams), and poetic. Cosmic symbols, which appeared in some of the children's responses have, according to Ricoeur, developed because humans first read the sacred on some aspect of the world or the heavens, such as sun, water, vegetation. The analysis of symbols through language allows one to express the sacred in one's own nature through deciphering the sacred nature of the world (1967). Children's symbolic representations can enhance their spiritual connectedness with themselves, the world and the transcendent (Relational Consciousness) through the universality of (archetypal) experience, and exploring their symbols can help them develop the meaning-making dimensions of their spirituality.

Three themes which appeared to function as recurring symbols in this research (Moriarty, 2008), were snake, which appeared in some children's personal stories and dreams, and island and mountain, which mainly appeared in the children's drawings on the theme of Journey, or Quest. In this chapter examples of two of the symbols are summarised.

Snake

In classical mythology the serpent is basically a life-force. It can be a symbol of mythic ancestors (as in the Australian Aborigines' Rainbow Serpent), a healer and seer, a source of fertility, or a tempter to evil (Cirlot, 1971). For children in Australia, where there are few dangerous creatures, snakes seem to symbolise something both dangerous and fascinating. A number of the children in the rural school mentioned snakes, which were part of their environment. The following is a summary of their "stories" about snakes, taken from their profiles and transcripts.

Bailey told a story of a television program where a meerkat "got bitten by a puff adder, and the venom did something to him, and the flesh was rotting away. And he survived!" Jacob discussed the snakes on his farm. He said he was afraid of "poisonous things like snakes". The family kills them if they come around the house or yard, but not if they are in the paddocks. He said, "We always run over them, and then we stop and have a look at them. There was a big brown snake (recently)". Jacob wants to live in the city "away from poisons". Luke related a dream about snakes on two occasions. He said "I dreamed that we were killing snakes, and we thought there was a dead one. And then we carried it to the barbeque, and then I saw it open its eyes, and then it came after us". Luke's dream and Jacob's story suggested that snakes were predominantly symbols of death for these children, but in Bailey's and Luke's stories, and others not recorded here, there were hints of the serpent being a symbol of life or rebirth, (where the snake came back to life) or fascination and temptation. For these children, the snake appeared to be a symbol which enabled them to explore the existential mysteries of life and death, of good and evil.

Mountain

Different meanings of the symbolism of mountain stem from its shape and height (Cirlot, 1971). Mountains, rising abruptly to meet the Heavens, form a symbol of transcendence, or the home of the gods in classical mythology. The ascent of a holy mountain is often seen as a way to purity or self knowledge. In Hebrew and Christian tradition there are many examples of mountains providing access to God, such as Mt Sinai, or the Mount of Transfiguration. In the modern world mountain climbers are revered as heroes who face great challenges to reach a physical and psychological summit.

Several children drew pictures of mountains, which seemed to have the symbolic meaning of achievement and self-worth. Luke drew his self-portrait with Mt Everest as a background. Luke was a very athletic child, always striving for greater physical achievement, such as in surfing or swimming. He said that his greatest achievement would be to climb Mt Everest. David, from the coastal school, drew mountains as his Journey picture. In David's picture there are tiny figures snow-boarding over large mountains. This gave the impression of human co-operation and achievement against the vastness of the natural world. David's concept of achievement through co-operation was also depicted in his self-portrait, where David was a small figure on the football field, working as part of the team strategy to achieve a goal.

Carmen, from the rural school, drew a picture of two figures in climbing gear struggling up the mountain together. This was her Journey picture. Carmen said the figures were people trying to break a world record for climbing "the highest mountain". She described how mountains were much harder to climb than hills because there were "rocks and stuff". She came from New Zealand where she had first hand experience of high mountains. Carmen liked daring physical activities, such as carnival rides, and driving her sister's car around the farm, where she lived in a rented house with her mother.

She wanted a motor bike, like her friends had. Carmen's symbolic mountain seemed to be more than a symbol of physical challenge. It may also symbolise a wish to climb out of the poverty trap in which her family was caught. Her mother was single, and earned a meagre wage, trying to earn enough money to buy a home for herself and Carmen. Carmen had two older sisters, who had left home, and were still socially disadvantaged. One of Carmen's desires was to meet her father one day. Carmen wanted to be an artist when she grew up, not just work in shearing sheds like her mother. When she was drawing her picture of climbing the mountain I commented "That's like life, a bit. Climbing to the top." Carmen smiled and said "Yes." Carmen's picture seemed to be not only symbolic of a desire to transcend her present social circumstances and achieve her life's ambitions, but also reflected her *sensory mode* and her *relational mode* in that the climbers, in their mountain gear, were engaged in physical struggle, but they were climbing together, helping each other get to the top. Unlike the children's stories of the snake, Carmen seemed to be aware of the symbolic nature of her drawing. It seemed to clarify her sense of identity as an aspiring achiever. It may also have given her a sense of her commonality with other "climbers" who were struggling to achieve a more satisfying life. Her drawing may also have been a sign of her connectedness to the physical world of her former home, and the sense of the transcendence that mountains inspire.

Transition or lack of integration

For the children in the study, reaching within themselves did not always result in integration between their outer experience and their inner lives. For example, like the rest of humanity, some had difficulty in reconciling themselves to the existential mystery of death. This was illustrated in recorded conversations with Lizzy and Luke, who were twins in grade three at the rural school. In their first interview, between just the two of them and the interviewer, they discussed the beginning of life on earth, as in the following transcript.

> W: (interviewer) How do you think the world began?
>
> Lizzy: It popped up (hand gesture upwards).
>
> Luke: I wonder what it would be like to be dead.
>
> W ... have you got some ideas?
>
> Luke: No
>
> Lizzy: (chants, smiles and waves arms) Going to heaven, going to heaven.
>
> W: Yes. What's heaven?
>
> Lizzy: Heaven is a place where all the good people go, and hell is where all the bad people go.
>
> W: I see. And what are they like?
>
> Lizzy: Um, like the leader of hell might be demons and the leader of heaven might be a really good person, like Jesus, God.
>
> W: (to Luke) What do you think about heaven and hell?
>
> Luke: (head down) I don't know. About the same thing.

In this extract Lizzy recounted the popularly held religious views about death and the afterlife. Luke, on the other hand, seemed to be preoccupied with the experience of death, and agreed with Lizzy reluctantly. In another part of the interview, Lizzy looked at Luke with disapproval when he did not agree with her account of Adam and Eve as the first humans. Subsequent material suggested that neither Lizzy nor Luke were able to reconcile what they had been taught about death with the reality of their experience of the recent death of their grandfather. Each one seemed to demonstrate internal tension about the topic in different ways. First is an extract from Lizzy's profile.

One of Lizzy's strategies for dealing with uncomfortable issues, like death, is by attempts at humour. In both of the group interviews, when death was mentioned, she started waving her arms up and down and chanting "heaven, heaven, heaven," "hell, hell, hell," and "grave, grave, grave". This in contrast with (her brother) Luke's quiet grief ... (However) one of her wishes was to never die, and to live into the next century.

Lizzy's response was very much in the *sensory mode*, with large physical gestures and attempts at humour. This was consistent with Hyde's (2006a) concept of trivialising, where he found instances of children avoiding the confronting of issues of meaning and value in life, and making light of such issues. In the group sessions Lizzy seemed to use this behaviour to distract the other children from a discussion which was probably painful for her. Lizzy did not mention her grandfather's death in any of her interviews.

Luke expressed his experience of death very differently, as indicated by this extract.

> Luke thinks about death, especially since his grandfather died a few months ago. When offered three wishes, his first was as follows.
>
> Luke: I wish my pop was still alive.
>
> W: Oh, How long ago did he die?
>
> Luke: I think it was June.
>
> W: This year! ... Ah, and you miss him?
>
> Luke nods.
>
> W: Tell me what was special about your pop.
>
> Luke: Most all the time I got to see him, and stayed at his house. Where my cousin lives.
>
> W: Was he sick, or just died?
>
> Luke: He was sick. We had to look after him. And he went to hospital. And then he came back and went again. And then he died (hands tightly pressed in armpits) on Sunday, when I

was in (a city 150 kms. away).

W: So, in the middle of the day?

Luke: Yes.

W: And what do you think has happened to him now?

Luke: I don't know (puts head down on the table).

Then followed a conversation about having pictures of his pop, and keeping him in his memory.

    Luke's experience of illness and death was very much in his *relational mode*. He shared with his family the anxiety of his grandfather's illness, and the details of his death. He experienced personal grief and loss, which he also expressed in the interview by body language, such as putting his head on the table, or tightly folding his arms, thus demonstrating his *sensitive mode*. His memories and photographs made him still feel close to his grandfather. However in his *existential mode* Luke placed himself at the intersection of a definite time and place. As he remembered his grandfather's death the time and the place where he heard of his death were significant for Luke. More significantly, he seemed to be trying to cope with the finality and the ineffability of death without the benefit of a religious faith. The earlier interviews suggested that he rejected what he had been taught in CRE (such as the historical existence of Adam and Eve) and embraced a spirituality which was focused on experience of the natural world, such as his profound experiences while surfing, and his joy in participating in sport. His Journey drawing was of himself against the backdrop of Mt Everest, which he would like to climb one day. This is consistent with Fisher's (2006) findings, that for young people, there is dissonance between what they are taught in school and what they believe and experience, particularly regarding the "God-factor". While Luke demonstrated more spiritual sensitivity than most of the children interviewed, his *nature mysticism* (Wilber, 2001) had not yet provided him with a rationale that could account for death. However, this dissonance, as experienced by Luke and Lizzy, could be viewed positively, as a possible transition to a higher stage of development of spiritual consciousness; as Wilber expressed it, from an "unconscious Hell to a conscious Hell", which may pave the way for transcending to a "conscious Heaven" (2001, pp. 48,49).

Conclusion

This chapter has described how the children in the study expressed their spirituality by "reaching within themselves" in a number of ways. The children utilised their own gifts and their spiritual sensitivities, and also resources available in their natural and social environments, to deal with personal issues and to become more integrated persons. Harry seemed to use self discipline and simple meditation, resources found in his community's Buddhist tradition, to deal with his anxieties. Grace appeared to utilise the assets of her relationships and her personal attitude to face her health problems with courage. These two children seemed to look within themselves to find spiritual meaning and hope. They also drew on resources in their social environment, such as their families' emotional support and religious faith. Other children exercised their personal gifts, such as sporting ability, imagination, or the ability to perceive their world through symbols, to reach greater spiritual awareness. These children seemed to be exploring their "being-in-the-world" as they integrated their imaginative experiences through books or television etc., and other people's perceptions of them, into a robust sense of their self-worth. They were also able to integrate these experiences to develop moral values and empathy with other people and the environment. Some other children seemed to be experiencing a transition phase, or contradictions between their inner and outer worlds, particularly in dealing with situations of loss in their lives. For example, Lizzy, and Luke, were struggling with the tragedy of death. Finn, seemed to be trying to reconcile his violent fantasies and his moral values, in an effort to deal with the break-up of his family. Even these children appeared to look within themselves to meet these challenges and to try to achieve inner harmony.

In seeking further understanding of this process of achieving inner harmony, the next chapter uses the metaphor of a map to examine the social landscape in which the children were growing up, and how they have negotiated their individual spiritual paths through that landscape. It does this by reviewing the children's values and aspirations, and how they develop within a social context.

Applications in the classroom

The findings in this chapter suggest a number of practical ways the RE teacher can assist children's inner spiritual growth. These are suggestions which utilise the *spiritual modes of being*.

- **Time for meditation or reflection in the classroom.** Although the time allotted for CRE is usually only half an hour, providing time for quiet reflection (perhaps up to five minutes) is time well spent. When children are calm and quiet they listen more attentively to the story, and reflect better on what the lesson means for them. They may even talk to God in their heads about it. This utilises children's *existential mode of being*, for reflecting on personal meaning, using their relation to time and space.
- **A supportive classroom.** This includes a range of strategies. The teacher needs to provide firm, consistent classroom management, where children feel secure. Praise for good behaviour from the teacher, and mutual support and cooperation among the children helps them to grow in faith in themselves, each other, and ultimately in God. This encourages the use of their *relational mode of being*.
- **Encouragement to develop all their gifts.** All their gifts and abilities come from God: sporting, musical, verbal,

imagination etc. Children can be encouraged to thank God for their gifts, and use them to communicate with God in their own ways. Inspiration they gain from their culture, stories, games, music etc., can be a channel through which God speaks to them. This is especially so for children who are not growing up with a Christian culture of the Bible and church. Children use the heroes, and significant interests and events in their lives to create meaning. Their own interests should be utilised to connect them to the Biblical narrative. This encourages the use of their *sensitive, relational and existential modes of being.*

References

Berryman, J. (1991). *Godly Play: An Imaginative Approach to Religious Education.* Minneapolis, MI: Augsburg Press.

Champagne, E. (2003). Being a child: A spiritual child. *International Journal of Children's Spirituality. 8* (1), 43-53.

Cirlot, J. (1971). *A Dictionary of Symbols.* (2nd ed.). (J. Sage, Trans.) London: Routledge & Keagan Paul.

Coles, R. (1990). *The Spiritual Life of Children.* London: Harper Collins.

Cooper, A. (1998). *Playing in the Zone: Exploring the Spiritual Dimensions of Sports.* Boston: Shambala.

de Souza, M. (2003). Contemporary influences on the spirituality of young people: Implications for education. *International Journal of Children's Spirituality, 8* (3), 269-279.

de Souza, M. (2005). Engaging the mind, heart and soul of the student in religious education: Teaching for meaning and connection. *Journal of Religious Education, 53* (4), 40-47.

Engebretson, K. (2007). *Connecting: Teenage Boys, Spirituality and Religious Education.* Strathfield, NSW: St Paul Publications.

Fisher, J. (2006). Using secondary students' views about the influences on their spiritual well-being to inform pastoral care. *International Journal of Children's Spirituality, 11* (3), 347-356.

Hay, D. & Nye, R. (2006). *The Spirit of the Child.* (Rev. ed.). London: Jessica Kingsley.

Heidegger, M. (1980). *Being and Time.* (J. Macquarrie & E. Robinson Trans.). Oxford: Blackwell.

Hyde, B. (2006). 'You can't buy love': Trivializing and the challenge for religious education. *Journal of Beliefs and Values. 27* (2), 165-176.

Hyde, B. (2008). *Children and Spirituality: Searching for Meaning and Connectedness.* London: Jessica Kingsley.

Jung, C. (1964). *Man and His Symbols.* London: Aldus.

Moriarty, W. (2009). Evaluating children's use of symbol in some recent research. *International Journal of Children's Spirituality. 14* (1), 47-61.

Mountain, V. (2005). Prayer is a positive activity for children: A report on recent research. *International Journal of Children's Spirituality, 10* (3), 291-305.

Mountain, V. (2007). Educational contexts for the development of children's spirituality: Exploring the use of imagination. *International Journal of Children's Spirituality, 12* (2), 191-203.

Ricoeur, P. (1967). *The Symbolism of Evil.* (E. Buchanan, Trans.) Boston: Beacon.

Salman, S. (1997). The creative psyche: Jung's major contributions. In P. Young-Eisendrath & T. Dawson (Eds.). *The Cambridge Companion to Jung.* (pp. 52-70). Cambridge: Cambridge University Press.

Snelling, J. (1992). *The Buddhist Handbook: A Complete Guide to Buddhist Teaching and Practice.* (2nd ed.). London: Rider.

Thompson, C. (2004). *The Violin Man.* Sydney: Hodder Children's Books.

Webster, R.S. (2004). Personal identity: moving beyond essence. *International Journal of Children's Spirituality. 9* (1), 7-19.

Wilber, K. (2001). *The Eye of the Spirit: An Integral Vision for a World Gone Slightly Mad.* Boston: Shambala.

Wright, M & Masten, A. (2005). Resilience processes in development: Fostering positive adaptation in the context of adversity. In *Handbook of Resilience in Children.* S. Goldstein & R. Brooks (Eds.). Retrieved http://www.springlink.com.exproxy2.acu.edu.au 27 July 2008.

5

CHARTING THE PATH:
"ROADMAP", VALUES AND ASPIRATIONS

Discussion – Social context of children's spirituality

The previous two chapters examined the children's individual spiritual responses to the world around them by looking outward as "Reaching beyond themselves", and looking inward for their spiritual resources as "Reaching within themselves". This present chapter uses the metaphor of a map to examine the social landscape in which the children were growing up, and how they have negotiated their individual spiritual paths through that landscape. It does this by reviewing the children's values and aspirations, and how they develop within a social context.

"Charting the path" refers to the way in which the children incorporated the influences in the society in which they lived, and how they envisioned their lives. This concept is developed from the literature of the concept of "worldview" in Erricker et al (1997), who described children's lives as narratives "constructed out of individual experience" (p. 9), which were used by them to construct "an evolving worldview" (p. 10), or "mental landscape, made up of many stories which give it meaning" (p. 12). Coles used a similar metaphor of "young pilgrims marching through life" (Coles, 1990, p. 320). This mental landscape is constructed, not only from the children's subjective individual experience, but also from the external landscape of their social environment. As Scott (2005) wrote "The spiritual will occur in a context of family and community influences, nested in the full range of ecosystems ... Any claims for the spiritual must be grounded in the full range of a child's experience and capacity, including their social systems and their interactions" (p. 195). Possible characteristics of Roadmap included "faith, moral responsibility, hope, joy". The findings of this research suggest that these characteristics may arise out of an interaction between the children's inner resources, as discussed in the previous chapter, and the contribution made by the children's community to their spiritual development.

My interest in the cultural influences in children's environment which shaped their landscape, and the values they acquired which helped chart a path of personal meaning in their lives, was stimulated by the analysis of the research findings. In the findings it appeared that the values which the children expressed, showed distinct characteristics in each of the school communities. That is, the values of the coastal, provincial, rural and suburban school children showed some distinctive features as well as ones they held in common. Although the research material on the communities represented by these schools was incidental and limited, (I was not consciously looking for it), I made use of this material. The primary material for this section was mostly obtained from the children's individual third interviews, which provided information about their values and aspirations.

Children's Values

Values Education has become an integral part of public, Catholic and independent school education in Australia, and other countries such as the United Kingdom, in the early 21st century. The National Values Forum Report: "National framework for values in Australian schools" (2005) commissioned by the Australian Government is one such document which addresses this issue. In the English context, Eaude quoted Halstead's (1996) definition of values as:

> principles, fundamental convictions, ideals, standards or life

stances which act as general guides to behaviour or as points of reference in decision making or the evaluation of beliefs or action and which are closely connected to personal integrity and personal identity (Eaude, 2008, p 59).

Eaude continued, "Values are formative and descriptive, aspirational and manifested in conduct. Values both reflect and structure beliefs, as well guiding and being exemplified in actions" (p. 59). "Guiding and structuring beliefs" does not necessarily refer to specifically religious beliefs, but any values affecting spirituality. Value-sensing was one of the key "categories of spiritual sensitivities" investigated by Hay and Nye (2006). Attributes of value sensing which these authors investigated were the emotional qualities of "delight and despair", the comforting experience of "ultimate goodness" first experienced as the child learning to trust its mother, and the cognitive and emotional process of awakening to "meaning" through life experience (Hay & Nye, 2006, pp. 74-77). Hyde (2008) further explored children's values and aspirations as expressions of their spirituality, particularly in his concept of *spiritual questing*.

During the interviews, information about the children's values and aspirations was mainly derived from questions about good and bad things people do, whether they have helped anybody or anybody helped them, and from their Journey drawings. The following are extracts from the transcripts of children at the provincial school.

> (Caleb was examining the picture of the refugees. He was asked what could be done to help them.)
>
> Caleb: Maybe (someone) could stop the war and end it for ever. I don't like (wars) because my grandpas, they both died in World War II. Maybe if I was a boy I could build a big war-proof house for them (the refugees). Or maybe I could make a war-proof shield for all of them ...
>
> W (Interviewer): Have you ever helped anybody?

Caleb: Well, in the playground, if somebody fell over and hurt themselves, when they were running away from someone, and they fell over a log, I would help them up and ask if they were OK, and tell the teacher.

W: Have you helped anyone?

Caleb: I have a play station game called The Fantastic Four ... and I helped (my sister) Alice, and showed her how to do it.

W: Has anybody helped you?

Caleb: When I was playing backyard cricket with Dad and Alice, Dad told me how to bat properly, because I was usually holding the bat the wrong way.

W: What good things do other people do?

Caleb: People in hospitals help people get better and help them have babies. The police officers, they can stop bad people, like if they robbed a convenience store, or kept a person hostage. And the fire fighters, they can help put out fires, and help cats down from trees.

W: What are some good things kids do?

Caleb: Do the dishes, clean up when they are not even asked to. Some kids help other kids.

W: What are some bad things that kids do?

Caleb: Bully, hurt other people, tell lies, be told to do something and they don't do it.

Caleb was quite an articulate child, and enumerated the range of values that were mentioned by other children. That is, he mentioned caring for other children, helping at home, and being aware of the needs of the wider community. Caleb's values seemed to arise out of his personal experience, as in his care for others who were hurt at school. The values that he had learned at home seemed to be about mutual help and about obedience. His values extended to the world beyond his immediate experience. They appeared to be informed by what he has learned at school and through the media – about hospitals and fire-fighters and criminal activities, and his family's experience of war. In other parts of the interviews he expressed the need to care for animals and the environment. Most of Caleb's values expressed his *relational mode of being*, in his sense of the importance of mutual care and respect for his family, friends and the environment. He also demonstrated care for the refugees, in relating their experience to those of his grandfather who died in war, and respect for people like fire-fighters who serve the community.

Grace described the mutual help she and her friend Peta gave each other. Grace demonstrated a high degree of empathy with her friend, understanding her friend's emotional as well as physical needs, that is, Grace's values were expressed in the *relational mode*.

> Grace: When Peta, when I fell over and I got this big, big scratch, and it was bleeding, she took me to the sick bay …. When Peta's upset I help her – because I say "What's wrong?" and "Has anyone hurt your feelings?" And she talks to me, and I say to that person, "You should be sorry, and you shouldn't do that again."

The children at the rural school also expressed most of their values in the *relational mode*. The following is a summary taken from Lizzy's transcript.

> W: Who have you helped?
>
> Lizzy: My little cousin … She was crying because we wouldn't give her a lolly … She didn't have money so she couldn't buy any … So I bought a bag for her, ones that she liked.
>
> W: And can you think of a time when somebody helped you?
>
> Lizzy: When I sprained my ankle at school. I couldn't get up. So my buddy (older student) helped me get up.

W: What does your family do to help you?

Lizzy: They can get things for you. They keep you warm. They do plenty of things.

W: What do you know about the good and bad things that people do?

Lizzy: The bad things are they steal, they rob banks, escape from jail.

W: You've been watching a lot of TV, have you?

Lizzy: Criminal Minds … Watching stuff. And the good things are they support you … If you are in a race they would cheer for you … (at school). They can play with you.

W: What about the environment? …

Lizzy: Give them (the animals) a better place. Yes, because there's water restrictions. And they should save the elephants, because there's not many Asian elephants left.

Mitchell expressed values of his rural community from a male perspective.

W: Tell me about a time when you've helped somebody.

Mitchell: (thinks)) My sister, she got her bike caught in another bike chain … I untied the chain off her bike, and got it out …

W: What about your family, what do they do to help you?

Mitchell: Help on the farm – loading … (My Mum) drives me to the bus (to school). She drives us to (town) for tea sometimes …

W: Tell me some good things people do, any people.

Mitchell: They help people when they're down (having a bad time).

W: What about at school?

Mitchell: Like help you with your maths questions.

W: What about bad things?

Mitchell: No rain.

Lizzy recounted examples of mutual help and concern from her own life-story. This was typical of the rural community. The children gave examples of caring for family members, especially younger siblings or relatives. They were aware of the physical support their family gave them, in providing food and shelter, siblings to play with, and a mother to drive them to the school bus. Mitchell was also aware of the emotional support that community members gave each other "when they were down". This mutual caring was also evident at the school. Lizzy and Mitchell mentioned peer support for physical and academic needs, and on the sports field. Some children were concerned with environmental issues, like care for endangered species, or providing feed for farm animals during the drought. J. Smith (2004) outlined a number of features of Australian rural culture which were exhibited in these children's responses. One of these ideals was "mateship" which had roots in the harsh environment of early rural settlement, and lingers today in male social dominance, rugged self-reliance, and the need to support each other in time of need. Rural females express support for their community by volunteering.

Negative features which Smith (2004) mentioned were rural decline in population and income, and sometimes, racism. These conditions were present in the rural school community and affected their values. For the children at the rural school, bad deeds mainly consisted of breaking school or family rules. Lizzy's consciousness of bad deeds in the wider world was what she saw on television. The effect of television, and computer games, was indicated in the enumeration of community "bad deeds" by other children. Carmen mentioned robbing banks, hurting people in the street, and breaking windows. The influence of the media was similar in all the schools visited. Kelly, at the provincial school, mentioned killing, stealing and raping. Finn, at the suburban school, was preoccupied with violent computer games and stories.

Responses of the children at the suburban school showed more diversity in their conception of values, just as their family backgrounds were more diverse and their community was less definable. The following two extracts were at the extremes of the range, for most of these children shared similar values of concern for other people. A general observation was that the children at the suburban school tended to offer more stereotypical examples than at the other schools, like "helping old ladies over the road". They also gave more examples of helping at home than at school, like cooking and washing up. Spencer mentioned that his neighbour had given the family a lot of practical assistance, like lending them his lawnmower. This might suggest that the school had comparatively less influence on values than the home for these children, when compared to the children from the other schools.

This extract from Tom's profile gives an indication of the complexity of his values.

> Tom's values and aspirations are interesting. He has some clear moral values. He believes that it is good to give blood or kidneys, and that doctors do good work keeping people alive. He is grateful when someone helps him. But he is struggling with moral ambiguity. He can see the good and bad features of graffiti. Graffiti is destructive of private property, but can also be worthwhile art and self expression. He told me about some friends in a country town, "and whenever they do wrong (their parents) would get a whip out!" I asked him, "Would you do that if you were a Dad?" He replied "No, I wouldn't do anything. I'd just put them in the room and talk to them". On the other hand, he sometimes sees violence as a solution. He would help the refugees by stopping the war. "I could get a rocket launcher and go pt, pt, 'Stop this war right now!' And it they don't stop I'd shoot them all." He mentioned other violent fantasies ...
>
> His initial response at times was quite materialistic, but it was followed by a different quality of response. For example,

when asked how the refugees would be feeling if their house had been burnt down in the fighting, he replied "They paid all that money, and then they lost all of it", but he went on "and they are feeling sad because to walk all that way with that much stuff would be very hard". That is, materialism was followed by real empathy. There was a similar pattern in his "three wishes". The first wish was that "I would be rich, and whenever I bought something my money would always stay the same". The second wish was "I wish all my friends could fly". This was so they could all have fun flying to school. The third wish was "I wish my family had a mansion for a house". As mentioned previously, his reason for wanting a mansion was "because it would be cool if we had a veranda and we lived right next to the sea. And we could look at the waves".

The following extract is from Hahn's profile. There were difficulties encountered in interviewing Hahn, which no doubt affected the material collected. She did not relate readily to the interviewer, or to the other children, and she had some difficulties with English.

Hahn ... seemed to value animals rather than people. "They don't talk," she said. She showed little visual perception when she viewed the refugee picture, but expressed sympathy for them as "sad" and in need of a warm drink and food, when the picture was explained to her. She could not recollect helping a person herself, but was aware of others helping her in practical ways. For example, her brother used to help her with her homework, and her father helped her mix the food for the dog and the rabbits. She could not think of good deeds in the abstract. Bad deeds included "somebody could kidnap you. They might take you away from your parents. And when you go to school people might harm you". This indicated a preoccupation with her personal safety, probably against a background of living in different cultures. Her wishes were to have more pets and more teddy bears. When it was suggested that she might like to make a wish for somebody else, she though for a while then wished that her sister could have a room of her own. Even this wish seemed to indirectly benefit her.

Tom's expressed values seemed to demonstrate a moral maturity in that he struggled with the ambiguity which is encountered in many adult moral choices, and Tom was trying to deal with hypothetical situations, not just personal experience. He was also aware of wider communal values, such as the virtue of organ donations. He also seemed to experience a conflict between materialism and altruism. His immediate materialist response to the refugees losing their house, their valuable property, was followed by empathy with their emotional plight. His three wishes also showed this vacillation between materialism and altruism. In the group interviews Tom did not demonstrate good rapport with the other children, preferring to pass on information rather than interacting with them. On the other hand he showed sensitivity to the beauty of his sea-side environment. Tom's valuing the beauty of the natural world seemed to express the *sensitive mode*, and in struggling with moral questions he was functioning in his *existential mode*, rather than the *relational mode*. Hahn also seemed to have difficulty in experiencing values in the *relational mode*, apart from her love of animals. Given the difficulties encountered in interviewing this child, it still seems that Hahn's values seemed to be largely confined to self-regard. However, consideration needs to be given to possible traumas that this child, or her parents may have experienced before coming to Australia from Vietnam, which may have generated her sense of insecurity.

Individual differences in development

Investigation of the values of individual children in the study highlighted individual differences in their modes of spiritual expression, and also differences in developmental maturity. The descriptions given above of Hahn's rather simple egocentricity and Tom's struggle with moral ambiguity are examples of such individual differences. There are limits to the capacity of Champagne's *spiritual modes of being* to explain developmental differences. However Cupit's (2007) Dynamic Systems Theory (DST) provides a credible and innovative approach to childhood developmental issues, and their impact on spirituality. This theory presents possibilities for describing the individual differences exhibited by children in this study. However Cupit's theory is complex and difficult to explain, so I will just refer to a few of its features. Some differences between children of the same age arise because of the effect of 'Agency', that is, the child's own choice to accept some influences and resist others. The twins Lizzy and Luke, from the rural school, demonstrated these parameters. While Lizzy's development as the clever, witty child, and Luke's development as the sensitive sports person could be ascribed to genetic and environmental factors, Lizzy's acceptance of conventional religious beliefs and Luke's rejection of them in favour of a nature based spirituality appeared to be the result of choice, or agency. Another of Cupit's terms is 'Attractors', which are forces within and around children which "push the child toward more developed behaviour", such as from crawling to walking. During a period of 'phase transition' the child's behaviour becomes erratic. Then it settles down around a higher level of development. Cupit described the following phase transitions which are relevant to the spiritual development of children in this study.

a) The emergence of language, with the ability to symbolise, organise and utilise information, which allows the symbolic representation of 'self' and others, of good and bad, true and false.

b) The ability to critically evaluate information for its truth and behaviour for its rightness, to judge and disagree with the ideas and behaviour of significant adults.

c) The emergence of personal autonomy (not social autonomy which occurs in late adolescence), reflecting the ability to formulate and maintain one's own position on important matters (Cupit, 2007, p. 114).

Some children's values seemed to indicate a stable developmental phase. For example, for Grace, mutual help was a strong and unquestioned value, and bullying and war were unequivocally bad. Hahn seemed to see moral values in terms of danger and safety. These children seemed to be operating in the symbolic phase described above. Other children in the study seemed to be operating in a transition phase towards more critical judgments. Lucy challenged her spiritual leader's belief in ghosts. Finn, as noted in the previous chapter, struggled to discriminate between different contexts of violence. While he enjoyed killing in computer games, he believed that it is wrong to kill real people, unless you are "an army man". Tom showed the inconsistency of a phase transition in his vacillation between materialism and altruism, as expressed in his response to the refugees. He also exhibited more maturity in his discrimination between different contexts for graffiti, and his questioning of the morality of corporal punishment in a situation other than his own.

This section was included to demonstrate that children develop along a variety of spiritual paths which are not accounted for by only one model. Champagne's *modes of being* are useful for demonstrating individual differences in the varied strengths of the sensitive, relational and existential modes. Dynamic Systems Theory, with its spiritual lens, is useful as an alternative understanding, which describes the varied influences of 'Systems Parameters' (the child's history), 'Agency' (the child's choices), and 'Attractors' (the phases of development during a child's life). This theory gives an added dimension to the understanding of children's spiritual development.

Children's Aspirations

This chapter looks at two aspects of the spirituality of the children in my study: their moral values and their aspirations for the future. The children's three wishes partly reflected their moral values, as in wishing for no lies or violent words, but more broadly their aspirations were for themselves, their families and the world. Examined school by school, these aspirations not only indicated the hopes and fears of individual children, but also their communities, and certain contemporary world issues.

Regional differences in aspirations

At the provincial school the main aspirations were for health, wealth, the environment, and a happy community. Health issues seemed to dominate the concerns of some. Alex wished that his mother would recover from her cancer (she has since died), Grace wished to be free from her asthma and eczema, Kelly wanted to be "born again" without bad skin, and Mary wanted "everyone to not get sick". Allied with this concern was a preoccupation with death. Kelly's first wish was to have Pete, her dead step-father, back again, and Ruth wanted "all dead people to come alive again". Other children's wishes were material. This was in the context of a school community where poverty was widespread. Billy wished to have a dog and to own their own house and have lots of computer games. Mary wanted everyone to "not run out of money". Jordan was concerned with acquiring consumer goods. An exciting moment for him was when his Aunty gave him a particular *Gameboy* (a type of computer game) he had dreamed about, for Christmas. Other children had wider concerns for the wellbeing of the environment and humanity. Alex's wishes were that no-one would steal and they would all be rich, and that no-one would hurt or annoy his friends, and they would be happy. Ruth wished that "all animals could live in peace". Caleb wished to help other people, for peace in the world, and for people to be nice to each other.

The children at the rural school had somewhat different concerns and aspirations. Some expressed personal aspirations for their adult lives. Olivia wanted to be an author, Kane a "house designer", Lizzy wanted to own a pet shop, and Luke wanted to climb Mt Everest. Some had aspirations to be wealthy. Bianca (whose family seemed to be affluent), and Carmen (whose family was not) both wanted to be rich. Bianca could not specify the advantages of being rich, but Carmen wanted her mother to not have to work so hard that she was tired and "boring", and to own their own house. Most of them had environmental concerns, especially wishing for more rain, and Kane expressed concern about pollution of the earth. Olivia wished for "no wars". This was in the context of the Iraq War being constantly in the news at that time. These children live in an isolated rural community. Their aspirations mainly reflected both local environmental issues, and thoughts about what they would do when they grew up and left the community.

The children in the suburban school were part of a diverse community, made up of some rather affluent traditional Australian families and a number of children of other origins, mainly Asian. Some of the latter families had been in Australia for some time and were reasonably established, and others had recently arrived and were struggling financially. A sense of all being Australian appeared to unite the school community. (This sense of all being Australian made a deep impression on me when I attended the school assembly, and witnessed the passion and beauty of their singing of the Australian national anthem.) The wishes and aspirations of the children who were interviewed were more diverse than at the other schools. Material aspirations were diverse in their expression and rather specific. Spencer wanted a new house and a computer with internet access, as he had quite recently arrived in Australia and his parents did not have employment yet. Harry wanted another computer so he did not have to share with his sister. Hahn, who already had a large number of animals at home, wanted more pets, and more teddy bears than her sister. Tom wanted to be rich. His family already had a holiday house, but he wanted "a mansion" beside the sea. He went on to describe the beauty of watching the sun go down over the sea. This suggested that there was a relational consciousness (Hay & Nye 2006), where children may relate to the natural world as the primary context of their spiritual consciousness.

Conflict was addressed in some of these children's aspirations, especially those who came from other countries, or who had experienced family upheavals. Lucy lived in a blended family. She wished that "everyone would get along and there be no fighting". Finn, whose parents were divorced, expressed this more broadly. He wanted "no such thing as war. That no-one ever hurt anyone, and no-one would say bad words". Spencer and Amanthi had come from a country where there was communal violence, and they wished for "no fighting". Harry's wishes were for the world at large, that "poor people wouldn't be left alone, and someone would come to cure their sicknesses". He also wanted to stop pollution, especially the pollution which happens in war zones. Pham's wishes were more personal. She wished to become a doctor when she grew up. Her specific wishes were that her brother would not be sick, that her dog would not wake her in the morning, and for a car with no roof. Other children had fantasy wishes too. Two of them wished to be able to fly, with wings. But Spencer wanted to be a pilot and fly jets. Lucy was the only one who wished that no-one would die.

The aspirations of all the children seemed to fit their individual stories, both their personal aspirations and their concerns for the wider world. Many of the children at the provincial school had experienced sickness, death and poverty in their personal lives. This was reflected in their wishes for good health and material security. Some of them were keen to acquire specific consumer goods. Their wishes went beyond themselves to include concern for the welfare of animals, a safe society and the health of the environment. The aspirations of the children in the rural school were focused on their need to leave their secure community when they reached adulthood and pursue a career elsewhere. The children at the other schools did not seem to have thought much about their adult lives, and they were absorbed with immediate experience.

Material aspirations

Material aspirations were expressed by many of the children, in a variety of ways. The threatened financial security of the rural children may also have been reflected in the desire to be "wealthy" as expressed by some of them. For Bianca, who went on expensive holidays, wealth seemed to express status, as she was unable to qualify why she wanted to be wealthy. For other children, like Carmen, Bailey and Mitchell, material aspirations seemed to be related to security, to have a home of one's own or for the family to be able to afford to feed their stock during the drought. It also impinged on their identity in relation to their peers, such as Carmen wanting a motor bike like the others, or not having to share the one family computer with all their siblings. At the suburban school materialism as an issue of identity was observed in some of the children. Hahn, who seemed to have difficulty in relating to other children, found her identity among her classmates as the one with lots of pets. She also expressed the wish to have more toys than her sister, perhaps as an expression of her identity within her family. Tom, like Bianca, was already well off, but seemed to conceive of wealth as a symbol of social status, or identity. These findings were consistent with Hyde's (2008, p. 147) observation that "this could be interpreted as children seeking identity and a sense of belonging through their material possessions". For other children, material aspirations were concerned with the struggles of daily living, such as needing a computer with internet access in a technological environment.

Family influences

Family stories seemed to be reflected in the children at the suburban school expressing concerns about the wider world. Their concerns about conflict sometimes seemed to be a reflection of their family story, as in the case of Lucy and Finn, and for some, like Spencer and Harry, this concern extended to the conflicts in war zones around the world. For Spencer this arose out of personal experience of conflict, and for Harry it seemed to have arisen from his grandfather's stories, such as having to wear a gas mask during the war in Vietnam. These children also felt free to exercise flights of fantasy with their "wishes". Lucy's wish to fly may have been just playfulness, or perhaps had some symbolic meaning of wanting to reach spiritual heights.

In a rapidly changing world, the home is still the primary instrument of socialisation for children, along with the local community and the media (Edgar & Edgar, 2008). The children were most ready to identify themselves and their interests with their families. By inference it could be seen that their families influenced their values and aspirations. Their attitude to possessions seemed to depend on the family's financial circumstances, and social status. Children of poor families seemed to be more concerned about the necessities of life, and also showed more concern for disadvantaged people in other places. Some children of wealthier families, such as Tom, seemed to see wealth as an instrument of social status and identity. This did not seem to enhance their *relational mode of being*, in that they did not seem to relate readily to the circumstances and needs of the other children.

Family structure was also a factor in their spiritual development. Many of the children came from intact and apparently supportive nuclear families. For Mary, strong family relationships were a source of gratitude, and enabled her to see herself as part of God's family. For some of the rural families, like Luke's, the father was often absent in employment outside the family farm. This was felt as a sense of loss. For Luke, and for many of the children, relationships with grandparents, and other family members provided security, and a variety of relational models. Grandmothers made cakes for them, and uncles took them fishing. For other family configurations the landscape was sometimes a little bleak. Kelly and Carmen had single mothers who experienced serial relationships. This encouraged Kelly to seek a sustaining relationship outside the family, with God, and her stepfather "in heaven". Finn tried to cope with his fractured family through fantasy, and he was sensitive to the pain of the refugees in their loss. In different ways the children's families affected their *sensitive* and *relational modes of being*. Generally speaking, the children who had experienced hardship, sickness or loss were more sensitive to others, as in their reaction to the picture of the refugees, than the children whose circumstances were more comfortable. In a more general way, experiencing home as a happy or a sad place seemed to affect their *existential mode of being* in the world. For example, Mary had a happy home for which she expressed gratitude, and sympathy for children who did not have "a mother and a father". Finn felt the loss of his father through divorce very keenly, and saw the imaginary world and the actual world as violent places.

Aspirations as "spiritual questing"

These children's aspirations were examples of "spiritual questing" (Hyde, 2008). The main themes of their aspirations were security, wider horizons and a clearer sense of identity. Aspirations for security can mean personal security (as in Hahn's case), or good health and security from poverty (as expressed by children at the provincial and rural schools). Questing for identity as Australians was expressed by children at the suburban school, and some children at the rural and suburban schools saw material success as important to their sense of identity. A sense of identity is an important aspect of spirituality, especially in regard to the relationship with the Self. This can be expressed as a relational mode of being. Tacey (2003) maintained that the Self only comes to know itself through the Other. He also maintained that "the self can be a legitimate doorway into the sacred" (p. 74). Identity can also be explored in the existential mode through seminal questions such as "Who am I? Why am I here? Where am I going?" Coles (1990) asked many of the children who took part in his research questions like these in order to explore their sense of identity. He saw them as young pilgrims on a journey. In their questing for meaning as family members, as Australians, or as investigators of the mysteries of life, death and suffering, the children in this research were trying to discover their place in a confusing and complex world.

Hyde based his concept of spiritual questing on Horell's (2003) exploration of questing post-modernity. Many scholars describe the "modern" world (roughly up to the end of the 20th century) as a time of relative certainty where people relied on a worldview based on science and the traditions of reason and Christianity. In contrast, in the "post-modern" world of the 21st century, traditional values are challenged, and people accept a variety of ways of seeing reality. Horell saw the main features of post-modern questing as moving away from a meta-narrative, or general world-view such as provided by organisational Christianity, to seeking spiritual grounding in the ambiguity and multiplicity of the influences of the 21st century. In a post-modern view, social identity is constructed out of a multitude of roles and influences to produce meaning and value. This scenario can be seen positively, as providing an opportunity for "imaginative creativity and the pragmatic construction of new patterns and self-identity" (Hyde, 2008, p. 91). For post-modern questers "the current milieu provides opportunities for a freedom to envision more life-giving and life-enhancing ways of being" (p.125). The children who took part in this research demonstrated spiritual questing in their concern for others and the world, and their desire to be part of a hopeful future. During the interviews some of them, such as Mary and Kelly, expressed faith in God and an afterlife. A number of the children expressed their sense of the transcendent, not overtly as in the Hyde study, but through symbols. The symbol of mountain, as aspiring for a better life, was expressed in drawing and conversation by Luke, Carmen and David. Lucy, Tom and Spencer all used the symbol of flying, which appeared to have transcendental dimensions for them.

Summary – A spiritual path

The values and aspirations of the children, and by inference, the communities in which they lived, can be an indication of their spiritual health. Crawford and Rossiter (2006), writing about teenagers, stated that "judging what is a healthy and desirable spirituality always takes place within a specific context where there are presumed values and beliefs, whether they are religious or not" (p. 198-199). Their criteria for evaluation include transcendent experience, frame of reference within a community, a sense of social justice, and being able to reflect on one's life and be open to challenges. All these criteria for healthy values were demonstrated by various children in my study. For example Tom and Kelly had a sense of the transcendent in their individual ways. Most of the children valued relationships with other people and the environment, and social justice. Mary and Kelly, for example, were able to reflect on and evaluate their lives. Some, like Alex and Jordan, were challenged by the mysteries of life. The challenge for religious education is to support the healthy values and to challenge less healthy ones, such as materialism and condoning violence. Wilber (2001), in searching for a balanced account of spirituality, gave the following definitions:

- spirituality involved peak experiences or a state of higher awareness, which can occur in any stage and any age,
- spirituality can involve a higher level of intellectual or

social development, or be unrelated to other levels of development,

- spirituality is an attitude (such as openness, trust, or love) that the self may or may not have at any stage" (adapted from p. 271).

The last of these definitions shows where values and aspirations are applicable to spirituality, which may be enhanced in an educational setting.

Religious education can encourage a balance between the three modes of being (Champagne, 2003) in children's lives, by helping to enhance other modes of being in individual children. For example, Tom, who showed strength in his sensitive and existential modes of being, could be encouraged to develop his relationships with others. Luke had strong relationships with the ocean and with his family, but he could be assisted to address his existential pain about the death of his grandfather. A number of children in the study, such as Bianca or Carmen, could be encouraged to develop their sense of self-worth, in relationship with themselves and with others, so that their sense of identity is less dependent on materialism. Finally, by enhancing children's being-in-the-world, they may be brought closer to knowing and relating to God (Champagne 2003, p. 52).

In this chapter the researcher has attempted to demonstrate the way in which wider conditions of the children's social and physical environments helped to shape their spirituality, in particular, their values and aspirations. There were differences in the values of the children in each school community. The children at the rural school primarily valued community solidarity and mutual help during a time of drought. The children at the provincial school valued physical and emotional support for their peers who faced sickness and financial hardship. At the suburban school, which was a more diverse community, the children emphasised their individual family's values.

However, the values they all held in common were care for other people – their family members, their friends, and people in others parts of the world – and care for the environment. They were also concerned about observing rules of good behaviour, in themselves and people in the community. The sources of influence in developing these values appeared to be the family, the school, and the media. The children's aspirations, such as desire for material wealth and status, concern for peace and harmony in the home and the world, and a healthy environment, also reflected their local community and their individual family circumstances.

Religious education in schools can provide an opportunity for children to reflect on their values and aspirations. While the influences of home, school and the wider media affect the greater portion of children's lives, the influence of regular religious education classes, under the influence of the Holy Spirit can, and do, affect the lives and values of many children, providing a powerful guide to those children who open themselves to its light.

Applications in the classroom

Religious education, whether specifically Christian, or multi-faith, provides a unique opportunity for enhancing and directing the development of children's values and aspirations in the following ways.

- Recognise that children already have a sense of right and wrong. "You don't have to teach children about fairness and unfairness. A sense of justice comes with the kit of being human" (T. Wright, 2006, p.4). This sense can be enhanced and directed through Bible story and Christian example.
- Balance between the different *modes of spiritual being* can be encouraged as the teacher gets to know individual children.

- Different levels of spiritual maturity among the children in the class need to be recognised, and respected.
- The variety of sources of children's values, home, community, mass media, and their own reflection and choices need to be recognised. Exposing children to a Christian, or religious, perspective can help children examine their values and aspirations, and aid their spiritual growth.

References

Champagne, E. (2003). Being a child; A spiritual child. *International Journal of Children's Spirituality.* 8 (1), 43-53.

Coles, R. (1990). *The Spiritual Life of Children.* London: HarperCollins.

Crawford, M & Rossiter, G. (2006). *Reasons for Living: Education and Young People's Search for Meaning, Identity and Spirituality.* Melbourne: ACER.

Cupit, G. (2007). The marriage of science and spirit: Dynamic systems theory and the development of spirituality. *International Journal of Children's Spirituality.* 8(2), 105-116.

Department of Education, Science and Training (2005). *National Framework for Values Education in Australian Schools.* Canberra: AusInfo.

Eaude, T. (2008). Should religious educators be wary of values education? *Journal of Religious Education.* 56 (1), 56-65.

Edgar, D & Edgar, P. (2008). *The New Child: In Search of Smarter Grown-ups.* Melbourne: Wilkinson Publishers.

Erricker, C., Erricker, J., Sullivan, D., Ota, K., & Fletcher, M. (1997). *The Education of the Whole Child.* London: Cassell.

Hay, D. & Nye, R. (2006). *The Spirit of the Child.* (Rev. Ed.). London: Jessica Kingsley.

Horell, H. (2003). Cultural postmodernity and Christian faith formation. In T. Groome & H. Horell (Eds.). *Horizons and Hopes: The Future of Religious Education* (pp. 81-105). New York, NY: Paulist Press.

Hyde, B. (2008). *Children and Spirituality: Searching for Meaning and Connectedness.* London: Jessica Kingsley.

Scott, D. (2005). Spirituality in young adolescents: Thinking developmentally. In C. Ota & C. Erricker (Eds.) *Spiritual Education: Literacy, Empirical and Pedagogical Approaches.* (pp. 94-108). Brighton, UK: Sussex Academic.

Smith, J. (2004). *Australia's Rural and Remote Health: A Social Justice Perspective.* Croydon, Victoria: Tertiary Press.

Tacey, D. (2003). *The Spirituality Revolution: The Emergence of Contemporary Spirituality.* Sydney: HarperCollins.

Wilber, K. (2001). *The Eye of Spirit: An Integral Vision for a World Gone Slightly Mad.* Boston: Shambala.

Wright, T. (2006). *Simply Christian.* London, SPCK.

6

FOOTPRINTS – IDENTITY

Introduction – constructing an individual identity

The previous chapter sought to demonstrate the ways in which social influences helped children construct a meaningful worldview. This chapter seeks to demonstrate something of the mechanisms by which the children in the study used the narratives of their lives to construct a meaningful identity, or sense of "who I am". Continuing the metaphor of journey from the previous chapter, the individual identity of each child is designated as his or her "*footprint*". I arrived at some understanding of the sense of identity of each child through examining all the transcripts of the interviews involving that child, and then constructing a spiritual profile of that child, as a summary of the material collected. At the end of each profile I asked the question "What is the distinctive spiritual strength of this child?" This appeared to me to describe his or her *footprint*. This process was similar to that outlined in Hay and Nye (2006). These authors identified "a fundamental characteristic of children's spirituality … a markedly individual character that seemed to reflect the unique disposition of each child" (p. 94), which they refer to as a personal "signature". They conceived of a "multidimensional characterisation of spirituality" (p. 98) of each particular child, in which his or her psychological make-up has a central role, along with other features such as age and gender. I also included broader features of the child's landscape such as family relationships, and the influence of the wider community. In my research a child's conversation usually contained no references to religious or transcendent subjects, such as God or heaven, yet I observed some kind of signature or footprint which expressed the unique spiritual style of each child, where his or her "spirituality" is described through Champagne's (2003) *modes of being*. Four of these *footprints* are summarised below.

Alex

Alex's *footprint* could be described as "speculating about the Big Picture". When Alex chose the picture of the earth from space, it represented for him "different people all over the world, different animals, different kinds of things they (children) might have – Gameboy (electronic games) and they could exchange them between countries". This led to his comment that "It's very strange, but I think life's a video game and aliens on other galaxies are controlling us". Alex also speculated about the origins of dinosaurs, and other features of the earth's history, like the development of the continents. Even in the events of his own life he tended to see a larger context. His dedication to sport was seen as opening up many possibilities. He said "you meet new friends, you learn things ... and because I might play AFL or World Cup or be in the Olympics ... You can become famous". Alex even saw a wider significance in being in a family, when he faced the possibility of losing his family (his mother was very ill), and having to fend for himself. He demonstrated a dark side of himself in dreams he related about him and his family fighting "millions of monsters", and not always winning. However he always remained outwardly cheerful.

Bianca

Bianca, from the rural school, was preoccupied with small things, especially with small creatures. On a visit to Fiji she was fascinated by small crabs. The features of pictures that caught her attention in *The Violin Man* (which was read to the group) were the pictures of little rabbits and a very small cat. She also liked looking after small children, especially her one year old sister. Bianca seemed uncomfortable when confronted with unfamiliar situations, like the interviews, or questions which were not concrete and specific. She seemed to be concerned to give a "correct" answer, and was reluctant to admit to using imagination or doing something unconventional, like talking to a dog. In the group interviews she looked to her friends for support. Bianca seemed to need the clear boundaries of the familiar, even when her family travelled. Her Journey picture was of an island paradise, but it had a very firm shore-line. She said that one of the bad things children do was to "go out of bounds".

Mary

Mary's *footprint* could be "the joy of relationships". Mary introduced herself to the interviewer as "a special person. I have a Mum and a Dad, and some people don't". She idolised her father, and valued the "family times" spent with her mother, two older sisters, and a younger sister, aged two. At school she had many friends, "practically the whole class". In the group interviews Mary demonstrated her friendship with Grace by offering her verbal and physical encouragement. She helped her friends, by standing up for them when they were bullied. She expressed her relationship with the earth, through detailing the need to care for baby birds, and to conserve water. Mary had some strong relationships with the transcendent. She believed in God. Her somewhat confused understanding of God was influenced by her concept of the family.

> God is in heaven, which is everywhere, so God is with us and taking care of us ... God made (the world) and Jesus, his son, and he looks after it, if he's not dead. And if he is it's sad because when Jesus, God, died, he put his son in charge, and

if he had a daughter he put her in charge after Jesus died and he would put his wife in charge if the kids were dead.

She prayed for relatives who had died. Mary told of being visited by an angel, at age 6, when she was in hospital. She trusted the angel to look after her, and was no longer afraid. Mary's personality had a dark side, as demonstrated by her Journey picture. She drew a busy road, with various children in danger, including herself. She also expressed a fear that she might die during an asthma attack. However, Mary's spiritual strength seemed to come from her strong relationships with her family, friends, the earth and the transcendent.

Harry

Harry was a complex character, but his *footprint* might be "drawing inner strength from the visible world". Harry reacted to the visible world with keen senses, an inquiring mind, and strong personal relationships. When he went to the park he liked the cool breeze in his hair. He loved playing soccer and other games with his friends. He watched his father repairing the car to see how it was done. He loved going fishing with his father and uncle, and eating the food his mother prepared. But Harry's dark side was a tendency to anxiety and bodily tension. His grandfather's stories about the war in Vietnam seemed to have made him aware of suffering and danger in the wider world. He got tension in his arms and neck at school, which he dealt with by doing stretching exercises. He also dealt with his anxiety by going to the park, sitting alone, and reading a book. He said "Sometimes I lie down and look at the birds and the sky. Then the wind blows on me, and cools me down". He thought about "waterfalls, water in a lake, or about the ocean and fishes". He also thought about "me and my dad kicking a ball around the park. Those are the things that make me happy". Harry demonstrated self discipline in his ability to internalise and draw strength from the joyful things he experienced in the external world.

Each of these children had a unique style for expressing their personality, and in particular their spiritual signature. Alex was expansive, Bianca needed safe boundaries, Mary had strong relationships, and Harry exercised inner discipline. Each child had a dark side of their particular fears and anxieties, and a prevailing spiritual strength. More broadly, these are a few examples of the categories of "reaching beyond themselves" in the cases of Alex and Mary, and Bianca, within her timid limitations. Harry demonstrated the capability of "reaching within himself", utilising his experiences of the world around him. These *footprints* demonstrate their spirituality through their *modes of being* (Champagne, 2003) in particular, their existential questions about their identity, as "who am I?" which was expressed in their individual styles. Alex expressed his sensitivity to, and relationship with the planet, and its different peoples. He was concerned with existential questions about his place in the universe and who is "controlling us". This filled him with both optimism and fear as he faced his family's uncertain future. Bianca demonstrated her sensitivity and relationship with small, manageable things. She seemed to deal with the big question of "who am I?" by setting boundaries within which she could be comfortable. Mary expressed her sensitivity in her perceptions of her relationships with her family, friends and God. Her existential questions were about what God and heaven are like, and how to face danger and death. Harry expressed his sensitivity in his relationship with the natural world, and how it could be internalised as inner calm for his anxieties. His existential questions about "who am I?" seemed to focus on the joy of being part of a family, and he was concerned about the existence of suffering in the world. The *footprints* of these children expressed their individual psychological characteristics: Alex's expansiveness, Bianca's timidity, Mary's sociability, and Harry's introspection. The *footprints* also seemed to be influenced by gender. Bianca and Mary's worldviews were very people-related. Alex and Harry seemed to be influenced by more masculine characteristics of focus on personal achievement and intellectual problems. As discussed in the previous chapter, their local school and community seemed to have an impact on their sense of identity. Bianca's life was bounded by her family and a small rural community. Alex and Mary lived in a poor provincial community, where illness and crime were not uncommon, and good things happened elsewhere, like through elite sport, or in heaven. Harry's family, and its Buddhist religion, and being in a school community made up largely of immigrants to Australia were safe havens for him.

The Role of Story

"Signature", as a clue to identity is useful for someone external to the child, such as the researcher, but the child's own sense of his or her identity is better accessed through story. The children in the study left their footprints through story. They usually did not tell long, coherent stories of their lives as an adult might, but they told many fragments of stories from their own lives, or from their imaginative world: dreams, stories they wrote, or stories recounted from books or television. These stories revealed to me, and sometimes to the child, significant clues about the spirituality, or meaning in their lives.

Conlon (1994) provided a useful analysis of the role of story, which could be applied to the children in the research.

Story provides a pattern of meaning, coherence, and unity. The story is the primary vehicle for revealing who we are. Human experience is best portrayed as a narrative. A good story rings true, uniting us to what is sacred. It reminds us of our roots and challenges us to consider our destiny. It increases our capacity for reflection and empowers us to engage more fully in life. When we tell or hear a story, two things happen: We are invited inside some-one's life, and we also open up to receive the other (1994, p. 10).

Telling the stories of their lives appeared to help the children, as well as the researcher, to find "meaning, coherence, and unity" in their lives. For me this involved looking beyond the four children already mentioned in this chapter, to include other children whose stories were recorded in earlier chapters. Finn's story of his holiday in Malaysia with his father and sister seemed to be a vehicle for exploring what was significant in his life. As he told the story to the group, and later to the researcher, his eyes were shining and his voice was animated. The family group met exotic and dangerous beasts, such as snakes and monkeys, and shared the discomfort of heat and sunburn. When the family was chased by a "dangerous" monkey Finn cried out "Dad! Dad! Dad!" Finn said, "And he picked me up … and he picked me up and we ran". This seemed to be a moment of meaning for Finn. His father demonstrated to him that he was loved. For a young boy who was grieving at being separated from his father, who now lived on the other side of the continent, this holiday with his father seemed to be a "sacred event" that showed Finn that he still belonged to his father. This trip also seemed to help him relate to other children better than was usual for him. He twice mentioned enjoying time at "the kids clubs" in Malaysia. As Finn told the story he was sharing something sacred with the listeners. In Conlon's words it empowered him "to engage more fully in life" (Conlon, 1994, p.10).

Lucy told a "journey" story of her trip to China which reminded her of her roots and may have challenged her to consider her identity as a member of both Chinese and Australian communities. She had an enjoyable time in China meeting her relations. Riding the "bumper cars" at an entertainment centre with her cousin was particularly pleasurable. She also told of the simple pleasure of going to the market on a hot day with her grandmother and eating ice cream on the way home. In her profile I noted the following.

> This is a child caught between two cultures: Chinese and Australian. Her family, her ancestors and her parents' homeland are important to her. Her recent trip to China was

a highlight in her life; she wanted to talk about it at length. Yet even within her family Lucy differentiated herself. She said she is different from her family because, when they eat at a restaurant, she likes her dumplings in the soup, and the rest of the family do not. She adores her cat, but her parents make her keep it outside, and do not provide veterinary care for it.

Lucy also explored her identity in the final interview, not so much through narrative, but through discussion and analysis, which fits her intellectual style. Here is a discussion about sport.

> W (Interviewer): Tell me about yourself. What you're like.
>
> Lucy: I'm short. I like sport, especially skipping. I don't really, I'm not really a football (Australian rules) type of person. Football's just OK.
>
> W: Is that because it's too rough?
>
> Lucy: Yes. And I don't like basketball because I get all scared of the ball if it hits me. So I don't like that either. And I think basketball is for tall people, and I'm really rather short.
>
> W: Do you like games by yourself, like skipping? (Lucy: Yes) Or do you do it with others with the big rope?
>
> Lucy: I like it because if I do it by myself I can do it really, really fast. And when I do it with other people I can sing rhymes with it ... I'm really good at skipping. I like roller skating. I think I'm good in science.

In this interview Lucy identified herself in terms of her body image and her competency. She was good at science and skipping. She also seemed to be trying to identify herself in terms of a sport that was appropriate for her. As noted in a previous chapter, sport seemed to be an issue for the children with an immigrant background at the suburban school, such as Harry and Spencer. Participation and competence in sport was a vehicle for identifying them to their peers, and themselves, as genuinely Australian. For some of the girls, Lucy and Pham, owning a pet was important, which was not part of their Asian culture, and seemed to be something that set them apart from their families as true Australians. Participating in sport and owning a pet were part of their story of being Australian.

Conlon (1994) elaborated on the role of story as a means of entering into the life of another as being introduced to a "unique human mystery", not so much providing a map as a compass, which points us in the right direction, for understanding the life of the storyteller. As previously mentioned, Bailey, from the rural school, told a story from a television program about a meerkat that survived being bitten by a snake. In telling this story he seemed to be identifying with the courage displayed by this little creature as something he aspired to. Bailey was "little" in the sense of being shy, softly spoken and not very competent, yet his enjoyment of imagining himself as James Bond in his video game, suggested that he compensated by having a grand inner persona. This inner life seemed to find expression in writing exciting stories. Bailey's stories point to a hidden facet of his identity as hero. They also helped him to interact and share his emotions with other children. This was evident in his animated contribution to the discussion of the television series "Meerkat Manor".

These are examples of the way in which stories gave the researcher insight into how events in the life of the child demonstrated, or even formed their identity.

Narrative Identity

While Conlon's concept of identity through story helped to demonstrate the expression and formation of the children's identity, the French philosopher, Paul Ricoeur's concept of "narrative identity" explained the process of forming identity through constructing a life-story. As discussed in a previous chapter, the children's own sense of identity did not seem to be fully formed, but a work in progress. One of Ricoeur's key ideas which are relevant to this issue is the concept of self-constancy. Self-constancy refers to the fact that when we ask of a person "Who is this?" we name that person (Ricoeur, 1985). Ricoeur goes on to ask on what basis a person is called by the same name "throughout a life that stretches from birth to death". His answer is that self-constancy, or "self-sameness" of identity throughout life rests on the narrative that a person makes of his or her own life, or others construct about him or her. Self-constancy is something that remains throughout one's life even when events and circumstances of life change.

Another of Ricoeur's key ideas is his extended theory of the phenomenon of time, and its relationship with personal narrative as recorded in his three volume work *Time and Narrative* (1983-1985). A brief summary was presented in Moriarty (2008), with reference to the present research. Ricoeur's described three categories of time:

- mortal or subjective time, or time as we experience it during our lives;
- the endless, anonymous cosmic time, or scientific/objective time;
- historical time, by which we measure and record time through "procedures of connection", namely, the calendar, succession of generations, archives, documents and other such traces" (in Muldoon, 2002, pp. 64-65).

Ricoeur explained that the writing of history, or telling one's personal life-story is possible because in the passage of time "traces" or remnants of that past are left. These traces may be documents or memories, which can give us links with the past through which causes of past events may be explored, or they can give us a sense of the human significance of the past event, as a sense of "having-been-there". In the case of the children in the study these traces consisted of their own memories of past events, or what they were told by family, teachers and others. The writing of historical narrative, or telling one's own story involves "re-figuring" (Ricoeur's term) the story to give it coherence, or to make sense of one's past life. This "re-figuring" also occurs when the historian tries to make sense of, or interpret past events. In this case the researcher tries to make sense of what she is told by the child about his or her life. The narrative reconstruction of the life of a person leads to some understanding of who that person is, that is it provides a *narrative identity*. Narrative identity can also apply to a group of people, such as "the ancient Egyptians", or "Generation X". The narrative identity of a person or a cultural group is both constant and changing over time, as the group reads the texts of its heritage, or an individual tells or writes his or her autobiography (Ricoeur, 1985).

In applying these explanations of Ricoeur, I gained insight into the significance of events which occurred over time for some of the children in the study. Through the telling of these events the children may have constructed their identity through narrative. Likewise, as a listener or reader, I, as the researcher, was able to construct an identity for individual children. This chapter explores the narrative of three children (Luke, Kelly and Aimee), where significant events in the child's life are re-figured by the child or his/her family, and received or "read" by the researcher, who developed a sense of the narrative identity of the child. In each case, the analytic process begins with a historical "trace", which is a physical event in the past, like a wave in the sea, or a birth or death in the family.

Luke

Ricoeur's concept of trace is illustrated in Luke's story, where standing up on his boogie board at age 3, has had the lasting effect of defining him as exceptionally athletic. Luke lived on a farm with his parents and twin sister, Lizzy. For the purposes of this analysis, Luke's birth was significant, in that Lizzy was born "10 seconds" before him. The re-figuring of the event of the birth of the twins by the researcher, and to some extent the twins, was as follows. Lizzy dominated their relationship as the older one. Her role was the clever one and Luke's was the sportsman. This is illustrated in an interview with the two siblings together. Lizzy held a rather light-hearted conversation with the interviewer about the beginning of the world, as she understood the Biblical story. Luke, on the other hand, wanted to talk about death, but his voice was not being heard; that is, until he adopted his given role of sportsman.

> W: How do you think the world began?
>
> Lizzie: It popped up (hand gesture upwards).
>
> Luke: I wonder what it would feel like to be dead.
>
> W: …. have you got some ideas?
>
> Luke: No.
>
> Lizzie: (chants, smiles and waves arms) Going in heaven, going in heaven!
>
> W: Yes. What's heaven?
>
> Lizzie: Heaven is a place where all the good people go, and hell is where all the bad people go.
>
> W: I see. And what are they like?
>
> Lizzie: Um, like the leader of hell might be demons and the leader of heaven might be a really good person, like Jesus, God.
>
> W: (Luke) what do you think about heaven and hell?
>
> Luke: I don't know. About the same thing.
>
> W: Don't you think about it much? Does Lizzie do most of the thinking, out of you two?
>
> Luke: Um, no (looks defiantly at Lizzy).
>
> Lizzie: Yes, probably.

W: (points at Luke) And you do most of the playing?

Luke: Yes (smiles).

Luke said he had to look after his mother, who had a medical condition. He was also solicitous towards his sister, who was smaller than him, less coordinated, and she had had a number of accidents and operations. He explained that a motor bike was too hard for her to hold on rough ground and that she had only started playing netball. This demonstrated another aspect of their differentiated roles, where Luke was the care-giver. It is not clear how much Luke understood this as his narrative identity.

A significant event for Luke was that at aged only three he was able to stand up on his boogie board in the surf. He was currently a keen surfer, and wanted to be a professional surfer when he grew up. Luke's feat at age three appeared to be a family narrative. While Luke seemed to have a mental picture of the event, which may be a genuine memory, it is unlikely that he remembered the significance of the event without it being recited over time by his parents. A more obvious example of family re-figuring of his life was the story of Luke climbing up to a cupboard, and swallowing a near lethal dose of medicine when he was one year old. During the interview Lizzy and Luke enacted the event of Luke rushing about frantically, bumping into furniture and walls because he was temporally blinded by his overdose of the medicine. This was a gleeful production, not a horrifying spectacle. This would appear to be a re-figuring of the event by the family, from a potential tragedy to a comedy.

Luke's narrative identity arising out of his surfing, and other physical exploits was to see himself as physically strong and a good sportsperson. His current experience in the surf had a spiritual quality, or being "in paradise" when he was within a wave. This seemed to be incorporated into his narrative identity.

Another significant event for Luke was the death of his grandfather, a few months before the interview. Luke's re-figuring of this event was to try to deal with his grief and loss. In the final interview Luke was "offered" three wishes. His first wish was "I wish my pop was still alive". He described the day of his grandfather's death a few months before, after a long illness. He used to spend a lot of time with his grandfather, and he missed him. I asked "What do you think has happened to him now?" Luke put his head on the table and whispered "I don't know". His grandfather's death not only left him grieving, but faced him with the mystery of mortality. The indications were that Luke's spiritual resources were in his relationships with his family and the natural world of the sea. As the earlier transcript indicated, he did not accept conventional religious beliefs. He rejected heaven and hell as "made up", and God had no relevance for him. He did not yet have a narrative that gave meaning to his grandfather's death.

Kelly

For Kelly the most significant event in her life was the death of one of her step-fathers, Pete. Kelly's life was marred by problematic relationships with her family and her peers. In the interviews she alternated between confidential approaches and aggression toward the other children, and the interviewer. She complained that "mostly all the class" were mean to her. Her attitude to her family was ambivalent. She said "I like my family", and was pleased with the shoes her mother had just bought her, and the family outings to McDonalds. On the other hand she said, with a smile "I hurt Mummy a lot when I was born", and said "My father left me when I was a baby". She fought physically with her older sister, and her younger brothers were "mean" to her. On the other hand Pete was "like a father" to her, who cared for her when she was sick. However Pete got sick and died of "sun cancer". On two occasions she described his illness, and how she used to visit him in hospital and give him drinks.

Kelly tried to re-figure the story of her life and make sense of her relationships. She tried to make sense of Pete's death by describing how the hospital changed his "good" medication to "bad" medication when he was making good progress, so he died. She believed that Pete was in heaven, but somehow still nearby "keeping watch over us wherever we go". She summed up her life-situation as follows: "I'd rather be in heaven with Pete right now, in heaven and have a family, and see my great, great aunty, than be down here and get picked on". She also had fantasies about being like Princess Mary, or "God's daughter", to be bowed to and to have lots of servants.

However, Kelly had established a narrative identity which was not all negative and escapist, and had links with the transcendent. She thought a lot about heaven, which she associated with Pete and with God. "Heaven is actually the whole sky, everywhere, all the time. God is watching everyone, like all the relatives". She wondered what heaven was like, "Do you really see it? Do you walk around it?" God, for Kelly, was a benevolent being, who created the universe, and is "really, really good at it". This gave her a sense of personal destiny, in which God "created the whole world, and our mums and dads, because he made Mummy's mum to have a mum. If my mum wasn't born I wouldn't be here right now".

Kelly was able to re-figure these events of her life into a meaningful narrative of a person who, in spite of circumstances to the contrary, was loved.

Aimee

Aimee, who lived in a coastal town, had a view of past and future time which connected her with being Australian. An object of significance for her was Uluru. As she studied a photograph she commented that the rock is "huge, really old ... and has been there many years". She said "I always wonder how it got there because it's so big. And you can see spear marks. Yes, you can tell it's got tracks over it. Ages ago aborigines have been there." Aimee commented that the coastal landmarks where she lived were also very old, and "could be where aborigines came and lived". Besides a connection with the land, Aimee also indicated a sense of Australia's "European" history.

> Aimee: I like imagining things that happened in literature …. like I imagine how people would have felt in the war, when they found out that someone might have got killed or something. And in the future something that could happen, to me and stuff.
>
> W: Why do you think about bad things that happen in wars and things?
>
> Aimee: Because I think it's quite sad that they do this for Australia and they got killed doing it.

Aimee had two grandfathers who served in the Second World War, which may have been a source of oral tradition for her. Aimee refigured these icons and stories from the past to fashion a spiritual connection with the land, and its history as an important part of her identity as an Australian.

Identity as a spiritual dimension

These three children were taken as representative of the process by which children in this research formed a narrative identity out of events in their own lives and past events in their families and communities. At the suburban school there were children for whom events which happened to their families before they came to Australia became part of their personal narratives. For example, Harry seemed to connect some of his anxieties with stories his grandfather told him about the war in Vietnam. Hahn's anxiety about being kidnapped may have had a similar origin.

The formation of a narrative identity by these children gives another perspective of their spirituality. Firstly, it illustrates again their connectedness, or *relational mode of being* (Champagne, 2003).

Aimee's story illustrated her sense of connectedness to the land of her birth. She demonstrated a spiritual connectedness to the physical features of Australia's landscape and its aboriginal heritage. She was also aware of the historical heritage of the great wars, which are a central feature of the Australia identity, as represented in the Anzac tradition. Luke's sense of self was also connected with the landscape, and the joy of his physical engagement with it through sport. Luke's sense of self was also intimately connected with his relationship with different members of his family, and his role as a family member. Kelly's story demonstrated her struggle to connect with her family and to establish her sense of worth. A significant event for her was her loving relationship with her step-father, and the sorrow she felt over his sickness and death. Out of that experience Kelly seemed to identify herself as part of a transcendent reality which included life beyond death, a sense of the love of God, and of her connectedness with a larger family of successive generations of the living and the departed.

A second feature of the spiritual component of children's narrative identity can be found in their *existential mode of being* (Champagne, 2003), in particular, the relation to time and space. This chapter has explored the relationship of some of the children to time; to events in their own past, past experiences of family members, and their historical heritages in Australia, or other countries. Significant space for the children in this research sometimes meant small spaces: such as Grace's secret place where she took "time out", and Mary's favourite place in the school yard, and Harry's place of peace under the tree in the park. In other instances significant space meant their home, or their bedroom (for Pham). Sometimes the significant space meant the school grounds, or the confines of the whole community in which they lived. This was particularly the case for the children at the rural school, where the school grounds and the district in which they lived provided the boundaries of their social networks within which they felt safe. For Bianca "going out of bounds" was considered a bad deed. For other children a landmark like Uluru, or the country of Australia, provided their sacred space. While no child mentioned a church or religious building, for Pham the Buddhist shrine in her home was a sacred space.

Van Manen (1990) discussed the phenomena of "lifeworld existentials", in particular, four existentials "that may prove helpful as guides for reflection: … *lived space, lived body, lived time*, and *lived human relations*. Experience of each of these "life-world existentials" enhances a child's sense of identity. Lived space refers to the world or landscape in which human beings move and find themselves at home. For the children in this research this lived space included the children's house where they lived, their country of birth or adoption, or a private space for quiet reflection. Lived space also included a sense of the bodies they inhabit and their capabilities. Lived relationships were also experienced through bodily contact and interactions with others, through which the children became more self aware (for example, as someone who helped or was helped by another child). Finally, through lived relationships, some of the children became aware of "a sense of purpose in life, meaningfulness, grounds for living, as in the religious experience of the absolute Other, God" (van Manen, 1990, p. 105).

Conclusion

Using the metaphor of a footprint, this chapter endeavoured to demonstrate the spiritual dimension of identity in the lives of some of the children in this research. Based on Hay & Nye's (2006) concept of "signature", the individual characteristics of some of these children's identities was described. The metaphor of footprint can be extended to take account of the "sand", or the social environment in which identity was "printed" by these children. The possibilities for exploring meaning, coherence and unity (Conlon, 1994) in a child's life through story were briefly explored. These were anecdotes from their lived experience, or from their imaginative lives, which gave the researcher, and sometimes the children, insight into their identities. Some insight into the mechanism of identity formation was explored through Ricoeur's (1985) concept of narrative identity. The interpretation of past events and influences in the lives of some of the children illustrated the way that they, and significant others in their lives, built up a coherent story of the shaping of their identities. These children's sense of identity was a further demonstration of their spiritual modes of being.

Relevance for religious education

Although religious education plays only a small part in the lives of most children, it can have a role in the shaping of their identity, or sense of self.

Firstly, this role will be different for each child, according to his or her unique personal "signature". Some children, like Luke or Alex, might be touched by the wonder of the realisation that God is the Creator, and holds a key to their intellectual and emotional questions about great mysteries of life and death. Other children, like Mary and Kelly, respond to the stories of Jesus' love to all people. Some, like Harry, Pham and Kelly might find in Jesus, a source of peace and inner calm. We do not know how and when the RE lesson will find a response, and we very seldom hear about that response. However, as we get to know our students we can develop sensitivity to the spiritual style and needs of individual children, and quietly respond in the way the lesson is presented.

Secondly, the experiences of an RE class, and its stories, can become part of the life-stories of the children. This usually happens in a gradual way. Older children or adults tell of how CRE was the place where they first came to a personal faith in Jesus. They might specify a particular year at school when this happened. Individual stories and lessons from the Bible can be incorporated into the narrative identity of a child. For example, for Australian children who already have a profound respect for the story of sacrifice like that of the Anzacs for "us", can link this story with the death of Jesus as sacrifice for each of us. The story of Jesus as the Good Shepherd may become part of a sense of identity as someone Jesus personally loves.

Thirdly, as well as significant times, RE can provide significant spaces and relationships for children. As discussed in a later chapter, the RE class can provide a space for quietness and reflection, or a place where a lonely child feels accepted, or where there is not the competitive pressure to succeed that happens in some regular classes.

The RE class can be a place for encouraging deeper relationships with themselves, others (perhaps with the natural world) and with God. It is our hope that being a Christian, will eventually become an identity for many children.

Application to the classroom

Religious education classes can provide the following

- Sacred story – different children may take in (incorporate) different Bible stories to become part of their lives, their identity.
- Prayer – RE teachers should pray for each child and each lesson, that the Holy Spirit will make the sacred story real to the children.
- Sacred time and sacred space – can be provided by the RE class, where children can encounter God.

References

Champagne, E. (2003). Being a child: A spiritual child. *International Journal of Children's Spirituality. 8* (1), 43-53.

Conlon, J. (1994). *Earth Story: Sacred Story.* Mystic, CT: Twenty-third Publications.

Hay, D. & Nye, R. (2006). *The Spirit of the Child.* (Rev. ed.). London: Jessica Kingsley.

Muldoon, M. (2002). *On Ricoeur.* Belmont, CA: Wadsworth/Thompson Learning.

Ricoeur, P. (1985). *Time and Narrative.* (Vol. 3). (K. Blamey & D. Pellauer, Trans.). Chicago: The University of Chicago Press.

van Manen, M. (1990). *Researching Lived Experience: Human Science for an Action Sensitive Pedagagy.* London, Ontario: Althouse.

PART 3

NURTURING SPIRITUALITY

7

Nurturing Children's Spirituality and Faith

Introduction

I have discussed what spirituality is, from various perspectives, and the particular characteristics of some children's spirituality in the 21st century. This chapter explores ways in which religious education teachers, and children's ministers, can help children in their care to grow in faith, and grow in wellbeing, to become spiritually mature and happy adults. This can be the aim, whether one meets with children as family members, or in church, clubs or any school, Christian or secular. However, this chapter will first focus on how we can nurture children's spiritual growth in the classroom setting in secular primary schools, or in Catholic, Christian and private schools.

Religious education in a secular society

The children in Western countries in the 21st century are growing up in a pervasively non-religious society. Even in faith-based schools many of the students live in families which do not practise the Christian faith, but the students attend the school on the understanding that they will participate in the school's religious program. However, teaching religious education in a state school presents special problems and expectations. In the state with which I am most familiar, The Victorian Department of Education and Early Childhood Development carries on a tradition which began in the 1800s, of providing education which was required to be "free, compulsory and secular". "Secular", at that time meant free from the bias of any particular Christian denomination. The modern definition of secular (Macquarie dictionary) is "relating to things not religious, sacred or spiritual; temporal; worldly". This is different in intention from some contemporary understandings which are best described as "secularism", or "a system of religious or social philosophy which rejects all forms of religious faith or worship". People who hold a secularist view are opposed to any religious teaching in state schools. However, there is arguably room for some religious content in that it can contribute to children's wellbeing, in a broad vision of education as one where "every Victorian thrives, learns and grows to enjoy a productive, rewarding and fulfilling life, contributing to their local and global communities" (DEECD, 2012). For example, one of the department's key responsibilities is to provide for learning and developmental outcomes. These outcomes include (for example) for children aged 0 to 8 that: "Children have the best start in life to achieve optimal health, development and wellbeing".

In most western countries there are broader aims for education beyond numeracy and literacy, which include an overall concern for the wellbeing of individual students and for their personal and social growth towards harmonious integration as citizens of the wider community. In the United Kingdom the current education act requires that:

> all National Curriculum subjects provide opportunities to promote pupils' spiritual, moral, social and cultural development. Explicit opportunities to promote pupil's development in these areas are provided in religious education and the non-statutory framework for personal, social and health education (PSHE) and citizenship. A significant contribution is also made by school ethos, effective relationships throughout the school, collective worship, and

other curriculum activities (www.education.gov.uk/schools/ teachingandlearning/curriculum, 25 August 2012).

In Australia there are broad provisions for the total welfare of students beyond formal academic learning. These are enshrined in policies like the Australian Government's "National Framework for Values in Australian Education" (VELS). This document sets out nine values which are required to be part of the ethos in all Australian schools: such as care and compassion, integrity, doing your best, respect, responsibility, honesty and trustworthiness. "Individual schools will develop their own approaches to values education in partnership with local school communities, including students, parents, caregivers, families and teachers" (VELS, downloaded 15/02/12013).

The role of Christian religious education

Genuine spiritual nurture of children requires more than teaching a set of values. It requires more than teaching information about religion, such as Christianity, although introducing children to its stories, customs and beliefs provides an important scaffold for the development of faith. Spiritual nurture must provide care for the well-being of the whole child: body, mind and spirit. Above all spiritual nurture must help the child to develop lasting relationships with the Transcendant/God, and other people and the natural world, and an inner life of comfortable relationship with him/her Self. This nurture does not happen in the classroom in isolation, but builds on existing relationships with the family, the school, the church or religious community, and the wider world in which the child lives.

Programs for providing Christian Education in public and religious schools seek to address the balance between providing information about Christianity and nurturing spirituality of children in a variety of ways. Christian religious education teachers, and children's ministers in any setting, have a desire that the children in their care should ultimately come to a relationship of faith in God, through Jesus Christ, and to grow in faith within a Christian community. However, the charter for teaching in state primary schools requires that we should respect the secular nature of that environment and the multicultural mix of students, and refrain from "proselytising" children. It is unethical in any setting, within or outside the church, to put pressure on children to "make a decision for Christ". It can also be counterproductive, unless the child is sufficiently mature to make an independent decision, not just to please significant adults, in which case the "decision" probably will not last (Ivy Beckwith (2004, p. 65). When parents send their children to a Christian or Catholic school, or a more traditional private school, it is generally on the understanding that they will required to attend religious education classes, and attend some form of worship service. The whole school ethos is intended to reflect Christian teaching and values. However, even in a Christian or Catholic school, putting pressure on children will not bring them to lasting faith.

Children are more likely to grow into faith in the context of a loving faith community, that is, with committed Christian family who are involved in a Christian church. This is not the case for many children in the average RE class, in a secular or religious school. However, there are often some children from Christian families, even in a CRE class in a state school, though they may not be identified. The RE teacher has a special privilege to support these children, not by singling them out, but by providing a personal model of Christian living, and a place within the school environment where the Christian faith is valued and supported. This can help children of Christian background to feel affirmed, and less isolated, and provide indirect support for them to share their faith with other children. Indeed, the RE class has the potential to nurture the faith, or the innate spirituality, of all children in the class, by modelling the faith, and by presenting the stories and the values which provide a context in which the faith of any child may take root and grow. Adults of mature years, as well as teenagers, have told me that their faith in Jesus Christ began through hearing the Good News when they were in primary school.

This chapter will deal with the following issues: the relationship between faith and spirituality, the development of children's faith, and how children's faith can be nurtured within a faith community (church), and in the school.

Faith and spirituality: defining faith

Karen Marie Yust (2004) reviewed different traditional concepts of faith, as faithfulness of a group of people to an agreed set of beliefs, or allegiance to a religious culture such as Protestant or Islam. Alternatively, faithfulness in an individual can mean acceptance of death as a martyr, or personal submission to a religious authority. Within these frameworks children can best be described as "prereligious" (2004, p. 3), since they are not mature enough to form independent opinions about the beliefs or allegiances of their community. These views make assumptions that faith is something external to the child and requires a certain level of intellectual and social development. However, Yust proposed the following definitions of faith, which can be equally valid for children as for adults.

- Faith is a gift from God.
- It is not a set of beliefs; nor is it a well-developed cognitive understanding of all things spiritual.
- It is an act of grace, in which God chooses to be in relationship with humanity (Yust, 2004, p. 4).

The view that faith is a gift of God and a work of grace is consistent with Biblical authority and Christian tradition. The whole Old Testament narrative is an account of the covenant relationship which God entered into with the people of Israel. In the New

Testament, St Paul wrote that "by grace you have been saved through faith, and this is not your own doing; it is the gift of God" (Ephesians 2:8). Many believers through the centuries have encountered God reaching out to them in unexpected ways, like the early Christian known as Saint Augustine, who met God in a garden. The reformer, Martin Luther, described a person seeking to live a spiritual life as *theodidacta* (taught by God) (2004, p. 5). The human response to God's gift of faith is faithfulness, which Yust defines as "a disposition that welcomes God's presence and seeks God's teaching" (2004, p. 6). Faithfulness is a transformed life which lives by the grace, or faith which has been given by God. Hebrews chapter 11 is a litany of praise for all the people of the Old Testament who lived "by faith", or a life of faithfulness to God. Since we have already established, in chapter 1, that children as well as adults are spiritual beings, it is open to all humanity to respond to God's gift of faith by faithfulness to God.

Faith does not come to children (and adults) only through their intellect, that is, through hearing and accepting a set of stories or beliefs, but also through their various senses and life experiences. Yust gives the example from scripture in the story of Moses and the burning bush (Exodus chapter 3), where Moses encountered God.

- Through the senses, in seeing, smelling, and feeling the heat of the fire, in hearing the voice of God and speaking in reply, and touching holy ground with his feet.
- Emotionally, as Moses responded with amazement, awe, and fear.
- Socially, as he responded to his name, the religious history and the present plight of his people. (Yust, 2004, p. 8, 9).

Through this rich, multisensory experience Moses' life was transformed to a life of faith and obedience to God's call. Later, this chapter will explore ways in which children can be given an opportunity in the regular RE classes to find some encounter with God's call to faith in various ways, and find their own way to respond. This is consistent with the findings of research in children's spirituality, that they respond through their various *"spiritual modes of being"* (Champagne, 2003).

Spirituality and faith: defining spirituality

Rebecca Nye is a pioneer researcher into children's spirituality, who with David Hay, initially used the term "Relational Consciousness" to describe children's spirituality (Hay & Nye, 2006). In their research they found that on some occasions children exhibited an unusual degree of consciousness or perceptiveness in everyday experiences which gave them "a new dimension of understanding, meaning and experience". This consciousness was relational in that it "added value to their ordinary or everyday perspective". It made them aware of their relationship with Themselves, Others, the World, and God. "In this 'relational consciousness' seems to lie the rudimentary core of children's spirituality, out of which can arise meaningful aesthetic experience, religious experience, personal and traditional responses to mystery and being, and mystical and moral insight" (2006, p. 109). Nye, and many other researchers, have concluded that children's spirituality is an initially natural capacity for awareness of

> the sacred quality of life experience. This awareness can be conscious or unconscious, and sometimes fluctuates between both, but in both cases can affect actions, feelings and thoughts. In childhood, spirituality is especially about being attracted towards 'being in relation', responding to a call to relate to more than 'just me' – i.e. to others, to God, to creation or to a deeper inner sense of Self. This encounter with transcendence can happen in specific experiences or moments, as well as through imagination or reflective activity (thoughts and meaning making activities) (Nye, 2009, p. 6).

Nye gives some hints on how to recognise this natural, innate spirituality in the children in our RE classes. We need to listen carefully to children's words, and not just to "correct answers". Nye gives examples of children referring to their experiences of God. For example the six year old child who said "I saw a star and I went to it and I saw God under the sky ... it was really nice ... sort of really nice and calm and things" (Nye 2009, p. 29). This example shows a child experiencing God through her imagination (a "real" experience for the child), and her sense of wonder and emotional response to the experience. It is important to be sensitive to the emotion, and the individual expression of a child, as a key to understanding her unique spirituality. Nye gives the example of a boy describing his experience of God as "this bishopy kind of alien" (2009, p. 30). Sometimes, as teachers, we need to talk less, listen more carefully, and value children's questioning and wondering, about special experiences, like seeing an angel, and also their more everyday experiences, like playing in the sand with friends, or wondering how the earth began.

Integrating spirituality and faith

A third perspective is provided by Joyce Bellous' (2006). She argued that every human learns to exercise faith from infancy as a consequence of learning trust in significance people, and a predictable world. Faith is trust in action. "People who cannot put faith in the predictability and orderliness of the world are unwell" (2006, 173). Faith has content in that one gives intellectual assent to deep assumptions acquired through life. Faithfulness is demonstrated in exercising faith or acting consistently on those assumptions. "Faith is an attitude which integrates the experience of a whole person" (2006, 173) in that it helps us to organise our perceptions of existence into a meaningful whole. A major influence in our organisation of reality is story: personally appropriating, believing and acting on the community's stories and beliefs. Faith is energy that permits an individual to develop a strong sense of self, and the integrity to chart one's own path in life. Faith is also what integrates a person into internal wholeness as part of interaction with, and commitment to, an external social environment. This is true of all people, whether religious or not. Religious faith, for Christians, allows both individuation and integration, and is the means for growth. This faith is an individual's confidence in God's saving power, based on the historical events of the Christ's life, death and resurrection. This faith enables integration into a meaningful life, as part of a faith community. Bellous maintained that every person, whether religious or not, exercises faith, to a greater or lesser degree, in finding meaning and connection "between what can be and what cannot be seen" (2006, 174). In summary, "believing is an outcome of faith ... it is the energy and the narrative that influence daily life. An essential human task is to learn to use faith in the right way, so that people can enjoy well-being, whether or not they put their faith in God" (2006, 174).

What is the connection between spirituality and faith? Both are essentially relational. According to Bellous, spirituality is a biological necessity, an ability to perceive what is beyond everyday awareness (cf. Hay and Nye, 2006). It is relational in that spirituality is a 'space' which for the young child, forms a bridge between the self and objects beyond the self. This is the psychological space where the organisation of experience into meaning occurs (Bellous, 2006, 176). However, the organisation of meaning for a child, or even an adult, is provisional, and referred to by scholars as "illusion", or imperfect knowledge. These transitional concepts about the external world, including concepts about God, are tested throughout life, for spirituality compels us to think.

> In its integrative role, spirituality forms illusion based identity through the construction of a mental mythology that acquires a quality of being, holistically conceived,

made up of insights, values and beliefs that give meaning, direction and purpose to life, including attitudes, emotions and behavioural dispositions that inform of ideals, beliefs and values about the self, others and the world as a whole that informs but does not determine action (Bellous, 2006, 176-177).

Faith, on the other hand, may be described as that which compels us to act. Faith is more than a disposition, for faith must have an object. It is through the agency of belief that a person puts trust in that object, such as God, and acts on that belief. Since trust is initially developed through early childhood experiences, a child needs the integrating activity of his innate spirituality, his thinking ability, to test his transitional "illusions" throughout life to come to a mature understanding of God. However, mature faith is more than growing maturity of understanding, it is also the result of "a real conversation" with God through the various experiences of life. "Faith education is grounded faith in the inner life to grow and flourish into healthy relationships with the Church and the world." (Bellous, 2006, 178).

Nurturing spirituality

Taking up the concept of Relational Consciousness, I will explore the nurture of children through their relationships:

- with Others and the World, such as with family, peers, community and the natural world,
- with God through stories in the Bible and other sources,
- with God and themselves through prayer and quiet reflection.

Nurturing relationships with others

Relating to the family

Many writers about children's spirituality (Beckwith, 2010) believe that children's earliest images of what God is like grow out of their experience of parents and other care-givers. Children who have a safe and loving home picture God as being always present, loving and caring for them. Through this experience they learn to be trusting individuals, and open to trust in God. RE teachers can encourage this positive belief through the many Bible stories of God's care for children: such as The Prodigal Son, and Jesus blessing the children. Jerome Berryman, in *Godly Play* (1999), constantly uses the image of God as "The Good Shepherd", through story and play, to allow children to explore their feelings about God's care for them. Students can be encouraged to talk about experiences of care in their families (without compromising privacy) to reinforce both this understanding of God and appreciation of the love they receive at home.

But what about children whose family experience is negative, even abusive? A girl said in my class "I don't trust **my** mother". This kind of information can be briefly acknowledged, and used as an opportunity to acknowledge that human beings are not perfect and some let us down, but Jesus is the Good Shepherd, God is a Father we can always trust. Catherine Stonehouse (1998, p. 129) gives an example of a rejected child who used to go to her room, and in imagination, talk to her "daddy king" who would sit her on his lap. In later life she realised that this was her experience of a loving Father God. Some children develop an idea of God as always punishing, perhaps for sins their parents don't know about. This can happen even when parents balance discipline with love, but perhaps the child does not have a sense of God's forgiveness.

The story in the RE lesson is an opportunity to ask children to recall family experiences of love, discipline and forgiveness to encourage them to relate their experiences to what God is like. But there are other ways the RE teacher can nurture children's relationships with their families, such as encouraging students to send home cards of appreciation, or other acknowledgement, such as doing special deeds of helping at home. The RE teacher can foster family relationships herself by praying for the families of the children, and by attending functions at the school where parents are present, such as sports days, or the Christmas concerts, and taking the opportunity to get to know the families where possible. Parents should be invited to attend CRE Christmas and Easter celebrations, or to attend an RE class to see what happens.

Relating to school and community

Children's spirituality can be nurtured by strengthening their relationship with their communities: school, church, and the wider world.

RE teachers can foster relationships with the school by supporting the values of the school, also by finding out what are the current topics in their curriculum and linking them where possible with the RE curriculum, and the Christian story. Children need to see that God's love for them is connected with all areas of life. For example, care of their bodies through good nutrition, and through sport, is showing respect for the lives that God has created. I have often heard children say in prayer "Thank you God that I am alive". Children also like to connect what they are learning, for example, to compare heroes in the Bible with sporting and other heroes in their contemporary world.

The most important relationships at school are with other children, and these relationships can be nurtured in a number of ways. This can be through applying values such as respect, and tolerance for difference as part of the general school ethos. RE also adds Christian values such as forgiveness, and humility, and gives meaning to the values they learn, as examples of God's character and his desire for us to follow his example, with the help of the Holy Spirit. RE can also provide a place of trust where children can discuss things that have deeper meaning for them. They should be able to discuss without embarrassment, spiritual experiences, such as seeing angels, or emotional experiences that they find awesome, puzzling, scary, or something that makes them really happy. The RE class should be a safe place where they can respect each other, and keep confidences. The RE teacher can set the tone by sharing her own appropriate experiences with the children. She can share such things as a happy or sad event, or an occasion where she was able to share an experience with God in prayer. Being "the God person" indicates our deep responsibility to mirror God's love to children by offering them respect, fairness, sensitivity and love in all our doings, both in the classroom and in the community where they see us. Adults have told me that they remember their RE teacher years before, who showed them something of what God is like. I met a teenager in the street one day, who told me that she began to believe in Jesus in my class in grade 4. She told me that she now belongs to a church and has been baptised. We never know what the outcome will be of building relationships in the classroom, with others and with God.

School is also a place for building spiritual relationships with people in need, and the wider community. These relationships can be nurtured as part of the general school program. The RE team can work with the school in providing help for victims of disaster, for Aid agencies at home or abroad, or for medical research, to name a few examples. If the school is not already running such a program, it can be initiated in the RE class, as part of teaching the value of care for others, and for learning various skills. One year my grade 5 and 6 class ran a "Beads and Beards" stall to buy a goat for an overseas Aid agency. The beads were a greater success than the beards, but the whole school supported their project. The RE curriculum also has places where we can invite an outside speaker, or show a DVD to raise community awareness. These are some ways to encourage care and concern for others within and beyond the home and the school.

Relating to church communities

Ideally, children and their families provide the best spiritual nurture within a worshipping community. This connection is more easily fostered in a parish school where the students are encouraged to enter into the sacramental life of the Church, or in a school associated with a particular church community. A church community is usually a total community, represented by all generations, and has a past history and a future hope. People are built up in their faith through a balanced life of worship, teaching and service to others; a total program for learning discipleship and commitment to the Lord Jesus and the kingdom of God. It is through relationship to Christ and each other that people, including children, learn trust and a sense of belonging, which are so important for well-being. In a church community children learn about their faith through the Bible and their Christian heritage. They learn a religious language through which their spirituality can be understood and expressed more clearly. Also, their faith can be critically examined and develop as they grow older. Yust summarises aspects of spiritual formation that happen within a Christian community as follows:

- belonging – an awareness that they have been "adopted", and loved by God and the community
- thanksgiving – learning to praise God for his goodness, and learning to depend on God for living
- giftedness – opportunity to develop gifts that God has given them
- hospitality – learning to care for others and act compassionately
- hope – an awareness that there is more to life than the

material world, and to be introduced to the mysteries of God and God's universe (Yust, 2004, p. 13-18).

However, the reality for many children in our schools in the 21st century is that their families have little or no connection with a Christian church. In our multi-cultural society many children belong to other religious traditions, and many families claim no religion. This presents two challenges. One challenge is to sensitively respect other religious traditions, while presenting the good news of Jesus through the Bible stories in an appealing way without any hint of pressure on vulnerable children. We should never try to recruit children to our own particular worshipping community or denomination. Many RE programs provide a block of lessons about the meaning of the church, both in the Bible, tradition and the contemporary world. These lessons should not be overlooked in the crowded curriculum, for they provide some understanding of what Christians do, and may stimulate children's curiosity to go to church and find out more. There are many stories of children going home from RE and asking their parents to take them to church. This has resulted in whole families coming to faith in Jesus Christ, and being incorporated into the church.

Another perspective on the relationship of children in RE with the church focuses on the initiative of individual congregations to connect with the CRE program in local state primary schools. All accepted CRE teachers must be affiliated with the Christian church. This places a responsibility on the congregation to sponsor their representative in prayer and financial support. These means of support should be the responsibility of the congregation as a whole, in public prayers and information. In order to be an effective witness to the children in her trust, the teacher needs disciplined prayer and the emotional support of other Christians. In addition to praying for the teacher's regular class, supporters can pray for each individual child on a regular basis. However this means that confidentiality about the child's identity and personal circumstances needs to be preserved. Some congregations have taken on the responsibility of supporting one particular school, and providing the CRE teachers for that school. The congregation can also provide interest and support for other enterprises run by the school. The local state school can be considered as a mission field in our own neighbourhood. Similarly, the Church or churches which sponsor a Catholic or Christian school have a responsibility to support the teachers and students in that school.

The other challenge for connecting children with a spiritual community is to provide a "church-like" environment in our classroom, a place where children are aware of God's presence. While a classroom is not strictly "church", there are some elements which can take on similarity. The first to consider is providing an environment of inclusion, love and trust, through the attitude of the teacher, in word and non-verbal communication. The teacher needs to come to the class in a quiet, prayerful, but enthusiastic frame of mind. She needs to show the children that she cares for them by respect, and personal interest, and thorough and imaginative preparation of the lesson. The essential elements of the lesson are similar to a worship service, in that the lesson can include songs of praise, prayer, "ministry of the word" through the Bible story, and (what is often missing in a Sunday service) time for silence and reflection. Nye (2009) summarises these features under the initials S.P.I.R.I.T., standing for Space, Process, Imagination, Relationship, Intimacy and Trust, as follows.

- **Space** – This refers to providing a sanctuary or sacred space where the children can sense that "God is here", and they are there to experience a different pace of learning. This is not easy in a classroom where there are visual reminders of the many activities that occur throughout the day. One way to "mark" the sacred space each RE lesson is to bring in a symbol such as a Bible, candle, cross, picture or something from nature such as a flower or shell which is put in a prominent place. Stories and prayers can be held on the mat at the front of the class, and the tables used for exploratory activities, and a corner (perhaps where the sacred symbol is present, or a set of coloured cushions to sit on) where individual children can go to be alone and quiet. The end of the lesson is marked (desacralised) by removing the symbol. The space is also kept emotionally safe, where feelings and opinions are always respected, and nobody invades personal space, physically or emotionally. The teacher can encourage space for silence, by setting an example of "talk less, listen more". For example, she can leave longer gaps of silence before responding to a child's verbal contribution, in case he wants to say more, or by respecting the child who does not want to contribute verbally.

- **Process** – Unlike most of the time children spend in school, where the emphasis is on outcomes of learning, spiritual growth is a process which usually occurs unseen and unheard. Children often expect that they must give the right answer, and be rewarded for their achievements. Nurturing spiritual growth needs to be different. Time needs to be allowed for quiet reflection, for exploring ideas through art and imagination. Time can be spent in being stimulated to explore deeper feelings and thoughts through open-ended questions like "I wonder what Peter was thinking when he saw the big waves?", or "I wonder why Jesus blessed the children?" As children grow older they should be encouraged to express their doubts and scepticism, as this is a part of growing into more mature faith. These questions are best dealt with, not by giving a definitive answer, but by throwing the question back to the child, "What do you think?" which helps him find an answer for himself.

- **Imagination** – According to Nye (2009) "spirituality depends on being open and willing to go deeper" in our experience of God, and understanding of ourselves and our relationship with God. Imagination and creativity are the natural way in which children deepen their understanding and experience. Young children learn about life through play. For example, they learn about nurture and care through playing with toy "children". Jesus very seldom gave a factual answer to a question put to him. He used his imagination in telling a story, and his hearers needed to use their imaginations to understand it. Berryman, in *Godly Play* (1999), reminds us that children need to explore the Bible stories over and over through their imaginations, through play, and through creative artistic expressions. Teachers can also encourage "off-beat" questions, as these can lead to new insights and deeper spiritual engagement. Berryman emphasised that the dynamics of a class time that nurtures the spirit is different from the class time in which lesson material is "transferred" from teacher to students. Godly Play sets up a "discovery" model which can be adapted from a church based setting to a school based setting. This can be achieved by allowing both teachers and students to learn together, through an attitude of reflection and wondering, which lets the story speak to each person, through the Holy Spirit.

- **Relationships, intimacy and trust** – are all linked. Spirituality is not just an individual phenomenon, it is also a communal, shared experience. As children in the classroom explore existential issues (about meaning in their lives), they are sharing their insights, their feelings, hopes and dreams with each other. They are learning together and supporting each other. The role of the teacher is to monitor such discussions to see that everyone is respected and drawn closer together, and that nobody's confidence is violated. One way to manage class discussion in a respectful way is to pass around an object like a "speaking stone" (Nye, 2009) to mark the person who is to contribute, either with speech or silence. Teachers and students learn the respectful art of listening. These are some ways to nurture spirituality by building up intimacy, and trusting relationships in the classroom.

God communicating with children – Through story

Christian Education Publications (2013, *Connect*, p. 8) provides a model of a circle of God's all-encompassing story. Within that circle are the overlapping circles of teacher's story, stories of other Christians, students' stories, and story from this part of the Bible (within the total Bible message of redemption). The model indicates that the best learning happens where all these stories intersect. This section recognises the importance of all of these stories, but concentrates on the interaction between the particular Bible story being told, and the children's stories. This builds on the body of research into children's unique spirituality, and the experience of others experienced in children's ministry.

Christians believe that the Bible is the key source of God's revelation of himself to humanity. Later revelation of God through the Church and its teaching builds on revelation in scripture. God's revelation through the Bible is a two-way communication process – God "speaks" and people "encounter" God. Most of the Bible speaks to us through story, the stories of God's dealings with Israel through their history, the stories about Jesus and the stories he told, and the story of the early church. About 80% of the Biblical content is story. The Bible has other kinds of writing as well – poetry and songs, laws and instructions – but they are all in the context of the story of God's dealings with humanity, and human response. Beckwith explains this phenomenon as "God knew there was something in the human spirit that could relate to, inhabit, and be transformed by stories" (Beckwith, 2010, p. 24). Some people are uncomfortable with the term "story", as it is sometimes used in the sense that something is untrue. For example, a child may be accused of "telling stories", a euphemism for lies. This is unfortunate, because "stories can and often do contain more truth about the human spirit and its relationship to the God of the universe than many factual treatises or propositional monographs" (2010, p. 25). We do not have many satisfactory "facts" or explanations about God that everyone can understand, but we all understand story. Jesus seldom gave an explanation in response to a question, for example, "Who is my neighbour?" Instead, he told a story of the Good Samaritan. The richness of a story like this is that every time we hear it we discover a new layer of meaning.

There are certain problems with the way we tell stories to children. There has been a tendency, for a couple of centuries, to believe that a Bible story does not have sufficient meaning in itself; that it needs to be explained, and we need to be told its moral or message. This means that "we've inserted into or infused these narratives with the truth we think they tell rather than letting God's truth spring forth from them for our own lives and peculiar contexts, allowing them to intersect with our own stories" (Beckwith, 2010, p. 25). The result is that we often take a linear approach to presenting a Bible story. We prepare the lesson with a particular stated aim, telling the story in a particular "interesting" way, leading the children to a particular interpretation which they then explore through various activities. This ends with a brief time of reflection to assess how well the aim of the lesson has been achieved. The time of reflection is then little more than a "show and tell" of completed activities. This linear approach to teaching a lesson is easy to prepare, and provides some security of routine for teachers and students, but children do not always learn in a linear way. They also learn through movement, emotions, intuition, and quirky imaginative engagement with the story, ways that allow the children to "put themselves in the story". Moreover, a "one size fits all" application of a story does not engage different children in their individual life-situations. It does not allow for the story to capture children in individual ways, encouraging them to be open to what the Holy Spirit wants to reveal to them in that story. Beckwith (2010) suggests a more flexible model – a wheel – where the Bible story is represented as the axle. Around the axle, like the rim of a wheel are the various activities used to engage children in the story. The spokes of the wheel are the conversations the class has about the story, arising from "carefully crafted reflection questions which grow out of the activities and the Bible story". This conversation allows children the opportunity to think about

- What happens in the story?
- What does God do in the story?
- Where would I be in the story?

This process leads children back to the "axle" or centre of the story.

Methods using story

Godly Play

Before discussing the practicalities of applying open-ended approaches which help children to relate to God through Bible stories in the school classroom I will outline popular methods used in churches, especially Godly Play (Berryman, 1991).

Features of Godly Play are the story told in language accessible to the children, and time spent allowing the children "develop habits of interaction and response to the Biblical material" (Nye, 2009, p. 66).

- The stories are told in a simple way, without gimmicks or embellishments, believing that the story itself has content which speaks to children's spiritual and emotional needs, such as identity, freedom, power, good and evil, love and care.
- The story is told slowly, and treated with reverence, so that

children can respond to more than surface detail.

- The story is told without a book, from the heart, with relatively few, but carefully chosen, words and phrases. Gestures, and appropriate emotional inflection of the voice, are used to mark important moments in the story.
- Attention is directed away from the story teller, by not using puppets etc., but simple images from the story. Pictures or model figures, are used to focus on the story itself.
- Using physical images encourages even non-readers to pay attention to the whole story. In Godly Play these images are usually a few simple figures (or pictures) representing the people and objects in the story. These are placed in the centre of the circle, or the front of the group. The children are then able to retell the story and explore it for themselves, using the simple figures or props. (Adapted from Nye, 2009, pp. 66-67).

Berryman's book *Godly Play: how to mentor the spiritual development of children* (2009) has much practical advice for Mentors in schools as well as churches.

Brueggemann's approach

Walter Brueggemann, a well-known Hebrew (Old Testament) scholar believes it is important to help children to appreciate the beauty and power of Biblical stories, much as they learn to appreciate other forms of literature. Children become immersed in the stories of their favourite characters in books, or on TV, film etc., (by dressing up as Batman, or a princess, or in the colours of their football star). In a similar, but more life-changing way, they can make a connection between their own lives and characters in the Biblical stories. They can learn to "put themselves in the story, listen to God's voice along with the characters and crowds, make decisions, and practice living the faith together with all those who have gone before" (Yust, 2009,

p. 42). Brueggemann proposed ways of linking the big picture of the religious story with the immediate experiences of children's daily lives (cited in Yust, 2009, p. 42). He believed that God connects with children through story in ways which potentially influence the whole of their lives. Here is some explanation of his five aspects of story linking. The material is largely taken from Yust (2009), as the Brueggemann book *Belonging and growing in the Christian Community* (1975) is out of print.

Five aspects of Story-Linking

1. Children **receive** the Biblical story of God's love and salvation from infancy through the lives and example of Christian parents and being brought up in the community of a Christian church. For most of the children in CRE classes contact with a Christian influence on their lives may be limited to contacts through a grandparent, or some relative or friend, and the influence of the weekly visit of the CRE volunteer.

2. Children can **hear** the story at home or at RE through reading or having a simple Bible translation read to them. It can also include children's Bible story books with pictures, other stories about Christian lives of famous figures or fiction stories involving children, DVD's such as the *Veggie Tales*, TV programs and other electronic sources, visits to a church or a celebration such as a baptism. Hearing the story is the central feature of a CRE lesson.

3. Children can **celebrate** the story by participating in Christian festivals, such as Christmas, by participating in public or church celebrations, or school pageants. In the classroom or at home, everyday events such as a child's birthday, going on a holiday, family illness or recovery, or even getting a new pet can be used as a celebration and reminder, perhaps with a Biblical story reference, that God

is with the children and cares for them. An occasional sharing of simple food and drink (subject to dietary needs) can be a powerful celebration of thanksgiving to God, and bonding with each other, reminding them of the Lord's Supper (the Mass).

4. By **telling the story**, or re-telling the story, children can make it their own. When young children hear Biblical words or stories for the first time they may repeat them by rote without understanding them. If we allow children to re-tell stories in their own words, they will interpret the stories through the eyes of their own experiences. As they re-tell the story to the class, or to listening adults, they are given affirmation and feedback which helps them develop a greater understanding of the story. Children can be encouraged to use their imagination to re-tell the story through many different means: through a drawing (individual or group), a game or comic strip, (which these days may be generated on computer), or a dramatisation, or even a rap song. Some years ago I gave some grade 5 and 6 children an extended opportunity to re-tell the resurrection story of Mary Magdalene meeting the risen Christ. Some did a group drama depicting Mary's fear and amazement, some drew a picture of the scene (such as going to the empty tomb), others found it difficult to connect with the concept of resurrection in Biblical terms, but drew beautiful pictures of flowers growing. It is important, as teachers, to allow children to engage in the story in their own way, without the need to seek approval for giving the "correct" response. Probing questions which help a child to explore her experience further can be helpful. Feedback from the other children can assist the re-telling of the story to become part of the child's consciousness.

5. **Becoming the story** is the ultimate goal of the process

of engaging with Biblical and related stories. We want the children to ask themselves what the faithful characters in the stories, for example, Moses, Mary Magdalene, Daniel, or St Francis or Nelson Mandela did, and how they can make these stories into examples for their own living. Some people encourage children to ask in their daily lives, "What would Jesus do?" Parents and teachers want children to grow up into compassionate and loving people. In a recent TV panel a diverse group of well-known media identities agreed that, as parents, what they wanted most for their children was for them to become "caring" people.

Applying principles of presenting Bible story to RE lessons

The focus is on the story itself as the message, and allowing for a flexible response from the students can make story telling more effective. The following suggestions are not intended to criticise or replace existing curriculum material, but to suggest ways to help further engagement of the children through enhancing the interaction between the Bible story and the children's stories. Most lesson material has a clear pattern which is easy to follow, and clear goals. This can be useful for focusing an RE lesson on a particular theme or value, and the place of the story in the whole Biblical framework, or the whole church-based curriculum. Having a stated aim at the beginning of the lesson gives it focus and structure, and helps to connect to a particular context in the life of the children. However, from the point of view of nurturing children's spirituality, this approach can restrict the impact of the story on individual children. Or, as Beckwith noted, "This type of lesson actually gets in the way of the transformative power of the Bible story … (For) every Bible story doesn't always mean the same thing to everyone every time they hear it. Bible stories, like all stories, speak truth to us in the particular time and moment in which we hear them, whether we are children, youth, or adults" (Beckwith, 2010, pp. 26, 27).

An alternative approach to preparing and presenting an RE session is expressed not as "The lesson is **about** the Bible story" but "The Bible story **is** the lesson". The children are able to put themselves **in** the story, by using all their senses to immerse themselves imaginatively and spiritually in the story. They are also invited to put themselves in the story through engaging their minds as they are asked some key questions. Regularly asking these questions can give the children a framework for understanding all the stories and their place in them. For example:

- What happens in the story?
- What does God do in the story?
- Where would I be in the story?

Some practical examples for the classroom

Planning the lesson time

1. Way in, connecting (5 minutes). Different curricula have different names for the introductory activity, but the aim is the same: to revise the previous lesson, and to connect the children's life experiences and interests with the lesson to follow. Some background information often needs to be given, such as where the story fits into the larger Biblical narrative, so that children understand the story better.

2. Focusing on the Biblical material. Prepare to tell the story by getting the children to sit in their "story place": such as in a circle, or on a mat at the front of the room. Older children may prefer to remain at their tables, but face the story teller.

I am using the story of Daniel and the lions (Daniel chapter 6) as an example of ways to use the Bible to focus on the children's individual responses to story, as the Holy Spirit may be using it to impact on their lives. It is possible to keep to a main theme of prayer, or of God's power to save, and yet allow children to respond according to the impact of the story on their own particular context and needs. Here is a suggested presentation of this lesson.

Prepare the story well beforehand, by reading the account in Daniel chapter 6 in a child-friendly translation. Tell it to the children simply and slowly, using simple figures or pictures to represent Daniel, the king, and the lions, finishing it where Daniel is rescued. Sometimes a simple refrain from the children, such as "he prayed to God", or a repeated hand gesture, can be used to maintain attention, but not to interrupt the story. In a following discussion of the story with the children, answer their questions, and involve them in the story by adapting the general questions above, to this story. What happens in the story? – What does Daniel do? What do his enemies do? What does the king do? What does God do for Daniel? How did Daniel feel? How would you feel if you were there? This could be followed by asking a child to act out part of the story to show how he would feel. Conclude by asking what this story tells them about God.

The children are then directed to go to their tables to work on one activity which allows them to express their individual response to the story. For example, some children might be impressed by Daniel's habit of praying to God, but others might want to follow the theme of being rescued from danger. The students can work on their theme individually or in groups. Group projects might consist of a play, a group artwork, a media report or even a song. Individual responses might consist of an activity in the workbook, making a lion mask or writing a personal prayer. Choices are limited only by what material the curriculum or the teacher has prepared, and importantly, the time available. During this activity the teacher moves around the class to observe and briefly discuss what each child is doing. It is not necessary for all children to complete the task, as some children might be spending time thinking quietly about the meaning of the story for them, perhaps in a Quiet Space in the room. If a child seems to be unfocused or disruptive he can be directed to a task in the book.

3. Reflection time

This part if the lesson is often rushed, and the effect of the children's engagement with the story is lost. Try to give 10 minutes to reflection and prayer. Make sure that the children are settled quietly, and learn to expect this to be a time of quiet reflection. For example, instruct them to sit cross-legged, with their hands on their knees. First, allow 3 or 4 students to present their activities to the class. This is not simply a "show and tell" session. It is an opportunity for them to demonstrate (with a little prompting from the teacher) what they have learned. For example, if a child has made a lion mask, let him wear it for the class. Then ask him, "Who met a roaring lion in the story? What did Daniel do when the lions roared? What could a child do when he met something scary like a roaring lion?" Accept the child's response as his genuine spiritual experience, even if it is not the "correct" one. For example, if he says he would not be afraid of the lions, mention that after a while Daniel wasn't afraid any more either, and ask "Why wasn't he afraid?"

This time is followed by a short, quiet gathering together of the children's experiences, followed by a short time of prayer. More will be said about prayer in the next section of this chapter.

Further examples of story telling

The same focus on imagination and reflection can be followed with older children, but for grades 5 and 6, the lesson may require a more intellectual, problem solving approach.

Responses to the story in Luke 8:4-15, generally known as the Parable of the Sower, can be both imaginative and analytic, according to the preferred style of each student, or group of students. The story can be introduced by bringing along four garden pots illustrating the story: a pot filled with stones, one with stones and a handful of soil, one in which the teacher has planted some weeds, and one pot with only good soil. Then the students can plant some quick germinating seeds (such as radishes) and watch what happens over the next couple of weeks. An analytic response is to examine the initial parable critically, as a teacher-led class exercise, using the coloured hats (emotions, information, negatives, and positives), to assess what the seeds (the message) represents, and why some seeds grew and some didn't. If not using already prepared material for the lesson the class may suggest categories for the interpretation phase of the parable, such as: Doesn't listen, Gives up, Gets distracted, Perseveres. Then the class can be divided into four groups to apply the story to imaginary children. What would a child who represented seeds sown in stony ground be like, etc.? This could be illustrated by group drawings or posters, or computer generated images. Again, it is important to leave enough time at the end of the lesson to reflect on what they have done.

This development of the lesson about the Parable of the Sower also conforms to Breuggemann's categories of story-telling, explained previously. The story is "received" by presenting the four pots, in the context of the year's curriculum which is focused on Jesus' message of God's love for us and our need to respond. The story is "heard" when told aloud, or through reading the parable together from the Bible. The story can be "celebrated" at some stage in the lesson with a song or prayer, or an action, such as placing a Bible in front of the candle (representing a response to the message of the seeds). The students "tell" the story back to the class through their artwork. "Becoming" the story is an outcome which may occur over time.

A lesson can be considered "successful" when students are engaged, and appear to find some personal meaning for themselves and for the class.

Children communicating with God – Songs

"Let the word of Christ dwell in you richly; teach and admonish one another in all wisdom; and with gratitude in your hearts sing psalms, hymns and spiritual songs to God" (Colossians 3: 16). In the previous section we explored ways in which children hear and respond to stories from the Bible or the life of the church, through which God may "speak" to them. A natural response is to express gratitude to God for his goodness, by singing praises to God. Young children love to sing. Older children are sometimes reluctant at first, but singing, or listening to others singing on their behalf through a recording, can become a natural part of an RE lesson. Songs provide a simple and effective way to remember a message about God. Children remember a song long after they have forgotten details about the lesson. Music is also an effective way to either begin or end a lesson.

Here are some practical hints for using music singing in the classroom. If the teacher can play a guitar or other portable instrument, and is confident in leading the singing, that is excellent. One doesn't have to be an opera singer, just be able to sing in tune. The teacher can bring a portable CD player to class, or download the music to play through the class sound system. Various curriculum publishers provide and recommend songs that fit the curriculum. These days many classrooms have a smart board and an integrated laptop. Words and images can be projected on screen to accompany the music. It is helpful to get the children to stand for singing, and use actions (or even dance) where possible, so that they are praising God with their whole bodies. Sometimes it is helpful for the children to sit, and listen quietly to music. Using music and song teaches children one of the basic ways to worship, through praising God, and listening to words that communicate God to them.

Children communicating with God – prayer

While singing songs is a familiar activity for most children, prayer may have to be learned. However, research indicates that young children may find prayer a natural activity. Nye quotes a five year old boy who said "I pray in my head, talking to myself and God whenever I'm lonely, every day really" (2009, p. 64). Vivienne Mountain's (2005) Melbourne research with children of various religious and non-religious backgrounds, found that all the children prayed at some time. Some valued prayer as a source of personal strength and meaning, especially in difficult situations. Some children valued prayer as connecting them with God and their religious community.

In my experience, prayer time can be the most significant time of the whole lesson. Most of what is learned in RE lessons will be forgotten, but if the children have learned to communicate with God, that will stay with them for a life-time. Even if other things crowd out knowledge about God, they will know how to meet with God at special times in their lives. Therefore, it is wise to not rush the prayer time, but to make it special for the children. However, some teachers do not feel confident in praying with the children. This chapter proceeds with some thoughts about the importance of prayer, and some practical advice.

What to pray

In public worship, and in many private lives, there are four main types of prayer which are meaningful for children. There are many models of these types of prayer in the scriptures, especially in the Psalms.

Praise and thanksgiving. Research indicates that children are naturally in awe of the wonders of creation and life, which can be directed to praising God for his creation. Children sometimes pray "Thank you God that I am alive". They will also spontaneously thank God for their family and friends, and for good times in their lives. A good way to encourage this kind of prayer in class is to ask "What would we like to thank God for today?"

Confession and forgiveness. In the classroom it is better to keep this prayer general. We can remind the children that we all "screw up" at times, or cause hurt to others, and that God is always ready to forgive us when we make mistakes or do wrong. The teacher can ask God for forgiveness on behalf of the class, and ask for help for all to do better in future. Sometimes the class can use a ritual, like writing something they are sorry about on a piece of paper, and burning it (outside and in a safe place). This can demonstrate that God "removes" our wrongdoing. Children can be encouraged to say the Lord's Prayer (which asks for forgiveness), or make a specific confession in private.

Petition and intercession. Children can be taught that God hears our prayers when we ask for something, but he only gives us what is good for us. They need to be discouraged from regarding prayers as a shopping list for self- indulgence or trivial requests (like "please make my team win this weekend"). If a child is going to pray aloud on behalf of the class, it is wise for the teacher to vet the prayer first, and give some guidance where appropriate. Children also need sensitive help to face the hard realities of life, such as, grandma might die rather than get better. One way to direct children away from the "Santa Claus" attitude to prayer to God, is to encourage them to direct their prayers towards concern for other people in need. Encourage them to pray for people in other places, as well as their own families.

Discipleship. This refers to prayers of commitment, and prayers for help to live God's way. They are reminders to Christians, and people of other faiths, of our daily relationship with God. Although many children in the RE class are not ready to make that kind of commitment, they can be introduced to believers' understanding of that relationship through The Lord's Prayer, and other traditional prayers of the church. Traditional prayers provide a formula, on which children can compose their own prayers to be said regularly, at home or in class. If the children learn the Lord's Prayer in class, and have it explained to them, they may gain an understanding of the blessings of a relationship with God, which asks for God's will to be done in the world. This includes committing our needs and the needs of others to God for help. Prayers of discipleship can help children to experience the connection between relationship with God and living God's way.

Lament. This kind of prayer is common in scripture, especially in the Psalms, for example, Psalm 13. This psalm could be introduced to children as a model, as it does not call for revenge on one's enemies, like some other psalms of lament. Yust (2004) analyses and explains prayers of lament in some depth. It is probably sufficient for primary school children to know that relating to God in prayer means trusting God, even with our complaints. We can confidently tell God our complaints, and the injustices we and others feel, knowing that God understands and will help us in time of need. Then we can thank God for his help and his love.

How to pray

Prayer can be part of the lesson at any point – at the beginning, middle or end. A prayer can be at the beginning of the lesson, where the teacher can thank God for being present in the lesson and ask for help to understand about God better. This can be part of helping children to enter a sacred space, something different from other school times. A prayer can be in the middle of the lesson, such as part of a meditation on the story, or a private prayer with an individual child in special need. Prayer at the end of the lesson can be a time to focus on quietness, and meditation. This will be explained in greater detail.

It is important that children should develop an attitude of prayer, by reminding them that they are talking with God, who deserves our respect as the creator of the universe. Insist on silence and stillness. Children should be told that they do not have to pray if they don't want to, but they need to be still out of respect for children who do want to pray. They can sit in a circle or with sufficient space between them at the front of the class, where prayer is usually preceded by a time of reflection on the lesson. Most writers on prayer and spirituality for children (such as Berryman) recommend that they sit up straight, with legs crossed and hands on their laps, and close their eyes. However, closed eyes are not essential to prayer and may make some children feel unsafe in a classroom situation. The teacher should not close her eyes, for reasons of safety in the class.

Prayer as silence

In the section "What to pray" I discussed various ways of talking to God in prayer. But for a real relationship with God it is even more important to learn to listen and hear what God is saying to us. For genuine nurture of their spirituality and faith, children benefit from times of silent reflection and meditation. This can be taught in the short time available in the classroom. Some Christians are wary of the term "meditation", which they associate with Eastern religions. But forms of meditation have been practised in the Christian community since the beginning. Silent reflection still forms a major part of worship in the Quaker tradition. It was also a Biblical tradition. For example, in Psalm 1, the writer describes the blessings that result for those who "delight in the law of the Lord, and on his law meditate day and night". In various ways, Christian meditation enables us to be still, and focus on God, so that we may grow closer to God.

People may be sceptical about children being capable of stillness and silent reflection. However, writers such as Yust, testify that in their experience children learn to appreciate and look forward to being able to be silent. Their lives are so full of activity and noise, that they have little opportunity to reflect on what is really important to them. "Children need times of intentional quietness and stillness to remain in touch with their spirit and the divine force that animates them" (Yust, 2005, p. 96).

Forms of meditation

Here are some simple forms of reflection and meditation which are suitable for children.

Meditation on scripture. There are a number of traditional exercises for meditating on a passage from the Bible. Here is one which uses the imagination to prayerfully enter into a Bible story. For example, the story of the Lost Sheep, (Luke 15: 1-7) is suitable for silent reflection. After the story is read, or told, the children can be invited to sit in the prayer position (cross legged, with hands on knees), and asked to imagine they are the shepherd, or the lost sheep, while the story is read again. Then they are asked to imagine a rough countryside, with lots of rocks and steep cliffs, maybe prickly bushes. Imagine how the shepherd feels when he can't find the sheep? Where does he look? How does he find it? What does he do when he finds it? What does the sheep feel? ... etc. Then the children can finish with a prayer to Jesus, the Good Shepherd, in their heads.

Meditative prayer. This model of silent prayer can be very effective in RE classes. Again, the children are asked to sit quietly in a circle or at the front of the class, in the prayer position. This model of prayer uses various sensory stimuli to focus the children's attention on God, or something within themselves. This has been used effectively with various imaginative stimuli in grades 3 to 6. For example, rather than asking the children to shut their eyes, ask them to focus on a visual object in the centre of the space, such as a candle, a cross, or something else relevant to the lesson just concluding. While looking at this object, ask them to say a prayer to God in their heads about the lesson, or something on their minds. If anyone doesn't want to pray he is free to think his own thoughts in his head. Other forms of stimuli include the various arts – music, pictures, poetry, etc. – which can all be effective for guiding silent prayer. A variety of musical genre can be used for inspiration, from popular gospel music to classics, such as the popular Pachelbel's canon. Sometimes children can be taken on an imaginative journey – to a place where they would like to be, or to a place where they might be in five years' time and have a decision to make. The teacher might ask "How did you feel? Tell God about it." The imaginative journey might be through places where Jesus went, as outlined in the previous section.

Centring Prayer. This is a form of intentional silence, during which distracting noise is shut out so that people can focus on God, or the spirit within them. This is achieved by sitting in the prayer position with the eyes closed, and practising slow breathing, in and out, while repeating a word or phrase of their choice, slowly in time with their breathing. Words commonly used are *shalom* (peace), *Abba* (Father), or phrases like "Jesus loves me, this I know", "God is great, God is good", or for children who do not want to use specifically Christian words, they can chose a word or phrase about nature, or from another religious tradition. I personally like to use a repetitive song, like those of the Taize Community, for example:

> O Lord hear my prayer, O Lord hear my prayer,
> When I call, answer me.
> O Lord hear my prayer, O Lord hear my prayer,
> Come and listen to me.

Centring prayer follows four stages.

1. **Preparing.** Choose a sacred word or phrase as the symbol of your desire to welcome God's presence and action within you.

2. **Centring**. Repeat that word or phrase to focus your attention on God.
3. **Dealing with distraction**. As you become aware of extraneous thoughts, move yourself back to your chosen word or phrase.
4. **Returning**. Slowly bring yourself back to the world around you by opening your eyes and beginning to focus on the space around you. (from Yust, 2005, p. 99).

Centring prayer is demanding of time and concentration, and is usually more suitable for regular times permitted in religious schools. However, with persistence, it can be taught in state schools. Centring prayer is valued by many adults, and can be of spiritual benefit for RE teachers for private prayer.

Closing prayers or songs

It is a good practice, especially with the younger children to have a goodbye ritual at the end of the lesson. This might take the form of a simple prayer, which might be given in the teacher's manual. Sometimes closure might take the form of a ritual, such as a song for saying goodbye to the RE time, even though the children will still be together for the rest of the school time. One favourite song, perhaps used with a power-point presentation of pictures, is the Irish Blessing;

> May the road rise up before you,
> May the wind be always at your back.
> May the sun shine warm upon your face,
> And may the rain fall softy on your field.
> Until we meet again
> May you be held in the hollow of God's hand.
> Until we meet again
> May you be held in the hollow of God's hand.

In conclusion the space can be de-sacralised, by the teacher saying goodbye, removing the sacred object (e.g. candle), and leaving the room quietly.

Conclusion

These are some thoughts about how to nurture children's relationships with God, through Biblical story and through prayer. The hope is that the children in our care will build an intimate relationship with God that will last them into the future, long after they leave school, and the lessons themselves are forgotten. They may come to know that God is always there with them, through the Holy Spirit.

This chapter has dealt with the nurture of children's spirituality through their relationships with others – family, friends, school and the community. This was followed by an exploration of ways of nurturing children's relationships with God, through engaging with the Bible and other stories, and through communicating with God through songs and prayer.

References

Beckwith, I. (2004) *Postmodern Children's Ministry: Ministry to Children in the 21st Century.* Grand Rapids, MI: Zondervan.

Beckwith, I. (2010). *Formational Children's Ministry: Shaping Children Using Story, Ritual and Relationship.* Grand Rapids, MI: Baker Books.

Bellous, J. (2006). The educational significance of spirituality in the formation of faith. *International Handbook of the Religious, Moral and Spiritual Dimensions in Education.* Vol. 1. Dordvecht, The Netherlands: Springer.

Berryman, J. (2009). *Godly Play: How to Mentor the Spiritual Development of Children.* Denver: CO: Morehouse Education Resources.

Christian Education Publications, 2013, *Connect: Lower Primary C2.*

Department of Education, (2013), Australia. *National Framework: Nine Values for Australian Schooling*. http://www.valueseducation.edu.au/values/default.asp?id=14515

Department of Education and Early Childhood Development, (2012), Victoria. http://www. education.vic.gov.au/department/Pages/default.aspx

Department of Education, (2012), United Kingdom. *The School Curriculum*. http://www.education.gov.uk/schools/teachingandlearning/curriculum/ a00199700/spir ... 25/08/2012.

Hay, D & Nye, R, (2006). *The Spirit of the Child*, (Rev. ed.) London: Jessica Kingsley.

Nye, R. (2009). *Children's Spirituality: What It is and Why It Matters*. London: Church Publishing House.

Stonehouse, C. (1998). *Joining Children on the Spiritual Journey: Nurturing a Life of Faith*. Grand Rapids, MI: Baker Academic.

Yust, K.M. (2004) *Real Kids, Real Faith: Practices for Nurturing Children's Spiritual Lives*. San Francisco, CA: John Wiley.

8

Maintaining a Balance

The purpose of this chapter is twofold. Firstly, because some time has elapsed since beginning this book it is advisable to introduce some more recent publications on children's spirituality, and their implications for teaching practice. Secondly, a well-balanced RE curriculum needs to address some other issues beyond children's individual and collective spirituality. Space also needs to be provided in the curriculum to introduce the basic teachings of the Christian/Catholic faith. Stories from the Bible need background information about their historical, geographical and social settings to be more fully understood. Children need some understanding of how individual Bible stories fit into the broad record of God's plan of salvation (Salvation History). Moreover, children need to be introduced to the beliefs, traditions and practices of the church, if they are to grow up as part of a Christian community. This applies to integrating children into any faith tradition.

Spirituality and Knowledge

A significant recent publication regarding children's spirituality is Ruth Wills' article *Beyond relation: a critical exploration of 'relational consciousness' for spiritual education* (2012). Relational Consciousness as a concept has been influential in the understanding that children are born as spiritual beings, since it was introduced by Hay and Nye in

1998 in *The spirit of the child,* (rev. ed. 2006). Children's spirituality is "conscious" in the sense that, regardless of their religious background, or lack of it, young children at times demonstrate an unusual level of awareness of the awesome nature of the world around them, and of a spiritual (transcendent) reality beyond the ordinary physical world. This heightened consciousness is "relational" in that it draws the children into deeper relationships with other people, nature, and the transcendent, and a deeper sense of morality and the meaning and significance of their own lives (2006, pp. 109-111).

Appreciating Hay and Nye's "relational consciousness" depends on some understanding of spirituality as an "ontological reality" (Adams, Hyde and Woolley, (2008, p. 14); that is, it is an essential part of who we are as human beings, and our oneness with all existence. This view that spirituality is a part of "being" is shared by philosophers such as Martin Heidegger, mystics such as Thomas Merton, recent researchers such as Brendan Hyde, and Elaine Champagne, and by a scriptural understanding of spirituality as the Spirit of God pervading human beings and all creation. Heidegger (1962) used the term "Dasein", which means "being-there"; meaning that humanity is an aspect of the existence of all being, not as separate beings. However, for Heidegger "being in the world" is also relational in that there is a "correspondence of being" and other human beings exist "alongside us". Hyde described "being" as "our way of *being in the world* ... and facing our tasks" (2008, p. 38). For Hay and Nye (2006, p. 134), "being" is primal: separate from and prior to "this and that" or "subject and object" (see Wills, 2012, p. 52). Champagne (2003), whose "spiritual modes of being" were the basis of my research analysis described young children as being spiritual beings simply by their *"being-a-child"* (2003, p. 52). These insights demonstrate the Biblical concept that we are all spiritual beings because God "breathed into us the breath of life" (Genesis 2: 7), and "all things came into being in him (the Word), and without him not one thing came into being" (John 1: 3).

This one-ness in being is not just a static reality but has implications for our relationships with other human beings, the whole, and God. In "being alongside" another, relationships are *immediately* encountered (Wills, 2012, p. 53). As Buber described this relationship: "when one's whole self connects with the world, fellow human beings and a transcendent Other (God), the relation is of "I and Thou" (Buber, 1970, pp. 56-57, in Wills, 2012, p. 53). The self's connecting with the whole affects all social relationships, and personal well-being. However, in practice this idea "I-Thou" relationship is compromised by what the Bible calls "sin". In contemporary Western society this is manifested in preoccupation with individuality and materialism (Hay, 2000). In his study, Hyde (2008) identified "material pursuit" and "trivialisation" as factors which inhibit children's immediate relationships with self, others and God. In Buber's terms, I-Thou relationships are replaced by I-It relationships, where the other can be observed or studied but is not encountered.

Wills (2012) raised a particular problem regarding children's relationship with the transcendent, and the implications for religious education. Firstly, she noted that Hay and Nye generally avoided using religious language when referring to children's spirituality, preferring to use secular language relating to innate spirituality. However, when writing about children's reported encounters with the transcendent, such as dreams about heaven, or meeting a "bishopy" kind of being, Nye tended to interpret these experiences through language reflecting concepts of a Judeo-Christian God. Secondly, Nye noted that as children grow older and learn about God, as understood in the Christian community, at home or at school, they tend to explain their transcendent experiences in established religious terms. This use of religious language has the effect of objectifying children's relationships with God, putting up a barrier. What was initially a child's experience of the transcendent/God through the senses and the imagination, a relationship of being, becomes a relationship of knowing, an I-It relationship with God, which formal theology tends to describe as a set of propositions about God. Wills (2012, p. 55) described this phenomenon as a change in "consciousness". A direct knowledge of the other is replaced by an indirect form of knowing. Philosophers, from Plato to Hegel and later, defined this indirect knowledge as "illusion", not in the sense that it is false ("delusion"), but what is incomplete, or provisional. As St Paul wrote "now we see in a mirror, dimly" (I Corinthians 13:12).

Based on the ideas of Hegel, Wills and others assert that it is the identification of illusion where learning begins (Wills, 2012). As children develop conscious awareness of their spiritual experiences, they are able use this awareness to critically examine inherited teaching about God. This can have a positive or negative effect for the children. In the present research it was a positive influence for Amanthi and a negative effect for Luke. Amanthi found that learning about Jesus helped her to relate to him, but Luke was turned away from believing in God by the teaching he received about faith and the Bible. The aim of enlightened religious education is that children will grow in understanding and faith out of a synthesis of their subjective, direct knowledge and the inherited knowledge of their faith community. The knowledge of their faith community includes knowledge of the beliefs, traditions and practices of that community. Religious knowledge, and its accompanying precise language, can enable children and young people to critically examine not only their individual spirituality, but also their place as developing believers, within the faith community and the wider world. Through religious education:

> children can be encouraged to wrestle with their own personal notions of a transcendent other against the backdrop of inherited or assumed conceptualisations of God in order to create a life giving, personal notion which does not remain static but grows and changes as mediation and contingency continue to influence (Wills, 2012, p. 57).

The role of religious education in the Christian faith (or other faiths) is not to treat children as empty vessels to be filled with knowledge that might bring them to faith. It is to provide the scaffolding on which their immediate but immature spiritual relationship with the Transcendent may be built into a mature, informed, but potentially personal relationship with God in Jesus Christ. St Paul described the desirability to build on the faith of a child as follows: "When I was a child, I spoke as a child, I thought like a child, I reasoned as a child; when I became an adult I put an end to childish things" (1 Corinthians 13:11). It is worth noting that in this context, Paul is writing about knowledge which is not merely external, but is a lived knowledge of love. Jerome Berryman, in *Godly Play* (1999) provided such an educational model, where introduction to religious language and Bible stories are a scaffold on which to build, through a time of reflection and play, when children can re-live the story (such as the story of the Good Shepherd) and integrate the story into their own, growing relationship with God.

The dark side of spirituality

Another recent paper which is pertinent to current religious education is by de Souza (2012) entitled "Connectedness and *connectedness*: the dark side of spirituality – implications for education". de Souza, along with other contemporary writers on human spirituality, believes that growth in human spirituality is along a relational continuum from a state of being alone/separate, towards deeper connectedness with self and Other, until a state of Ultimate Unity is reached. In this state of Ultimate Unity "boundaries between Self and Other become blurred ... (and) the individual becomes one with Other, Self becomes part of the Whole which comprises Other and the individual has entered the realm of Ultimate Unity" (p. 292). This concept is very helpful for finding a common understanding with other religions, especially Hinduism and Buddhism. However, my Christian understanding makes me uncomfortable with a view which seems to negate the ideal of a personal relationship with a Personal God. de Souza acknowledged this problem in her note (p. 302).

However, the understanding of spiritual growth as entering into deeper relationships is compatible with a Christian understanding of the Incarnation of God, in Christ who became a human being. This deepening relationship with God means a life no longer self-centred, but is deeply related to this world and its people. The Catholic mystic Thomas Merton, referred to in chapter 1, is an example of this phenomenon. The deeper his relationship with God, the more concerned he became with issues of justice in the world. I believe that Christian religious educators should take seriously the insights of researchers in the various academic fields of spirituality, and seriously engage with people and beliefs of other faiths, in a multicultural society. But ultimately we need to study Scripture and Christian traditions, and be true to our understanding of them.

But the main theme of de Souza's article is the need for education to address the dark side of human nature, if we are to help children to grow in their self-awareness or consciousness of themselves, and in their various relationships. Recent emphasis on spirituality has its positive aspects: such as connectedness, experiences of joy, compassion, freedom and self-transcendence etc (2012, p. 293), but often ignores the negative aspects of human personality such as: ignorance, aggression, jealousy, sense of inferiority, all the traits which harm relationships. In emphasising the light we may be ignoring the dark side of human spirituality. In Biblical terms, it is sin that separates us from each other, from God, and from knowing ourselves. The psychoanalyst, Carl Jung, believed that the human personality is composed of positive, acceptable features (the persona), and corresponding dark, unacceptable features (the shadow). Both the rational, moral part of us, and the bodily urges and the emotions are part of our total humanity. Repressing the dark features in the individual can lead to "neurosis", and in the public arena can lead to scapegoating, and bigotry and hatred of "outsiders".

Bingaman (2001) argues that Christianity has traditionally tried to discipline the shadow in us, by seeking to suppress our desires, passions and sexuality with the aim of becoming "Christlike", and living perfect, holy lives as "new creations". According to Jung (in Bingaman, 2001), this aspiration is not only unrealistic, but also leads to a split personality, where people may deny that their dark, inner urges exist, or project self-loathing, and blame them on other people or the devil. Wholesome, integrated, or "individuated" people recognise their own shadow side, and even embrace the positive aspects of our animal nature, with its instincts and creative energy (2001). Indeed, the struggle to integrate the anima and the shadow into a truly "whole" person results in spiritual growth. Jung stressed that it is important to "Know thyself" in every aspect of the human personality. "Jung's redemption of the human body, and the here-and-now of earthly reality, is nothing short of an affirmation of the totality of human existence, an overt and unequivocal *yes* to human life" (2001, p. 176). Bingaman (2001) explains this in theological terms as acknowledging that "the kingdom of God is within you" (Luke 17-21). That being said, Jung seems to not believe in the possibility of an ongoing spiritual renewal in this life, by the power of the Holy Spirit, not just by self-examination.

As part of my research analysis I made a profile of each child I interviewed, which included mentioning his or her dark side. For example, Mary's strength, or positive feature was trust, in her family and the angel, but her dark side was fear of physical danger and death. Harry's positive traits were that he was "intelligent, self-possessed, with a strong sense of his identity", but his dark side appeared to be anxiety and physical tension. Finn appeared to be a lively, happy child, but his dark side included loneliness and loss, and preoccupation with violent fantasies. Each of these children struggled to cope with their dark side. This gave me some indication of their shadow, in its negative and possible positive aspects. Mary's fear of sickness and death made her very supportive of Grace, with her health problems. Finn's preoccupation with violent games may have given him insight, to discriminate between legitimate aggression in a soldier, and inappropriate aggression toward his peers.

Education which addresses children's spirituality, whether in a religious or secular school, needs to provide space for children to confront their shadow. "It would seem that recognition of the shadow is vital if an individual is to develop as a whole person" (de Souza, 2012, p. 296). Words which describe the spiritual disconnectedness associated with shadow include: alienation, disenfranchisement, disenchantment, unhappiness, discontent, prejudice and racism, envy, feelings of loss and being lost, anxiety, boredom, apathy etc. (2012, p. 297). de Souza, and other writers, identify a number of features of contemporary life which prompt disconnectedness, and the emergence of the shadow in children's lives. Hyde (2008) identifies two features: preoccupation with material pursuits, and "trivialising", or "the avoidance of confronting issues of meaning and value in life" (2008, p. 149). A pervading feature of contemporary life is that adults' and children's lives are so busy, too taken up with "lifestyle" pursuits, to find time and space for quiet reflection and self-understanding.

Addressing children's dark side, whether due to their inner shadow, or painful external circumstances in life, requires not only time and space, but also a trusting and sensitive environment, where children can grieve or reflect in silence, or openly discuss issues which may cause them fear, anxiety or guilt. The present social and educational climate is not conducive to this kind of self-examination. At home and at school, many children are given unreal expectations: that they are always lovable, that they will never fail, they can succeed in whatever they want, all their material wants will be met, and they will never have to face danger or disappointment. As de Souza commented, "no wonder so many children today escape into a virtual world" (2012, p. 300) when faced with the harsh realities of life. Children need to be taught to be discerning; to accept their uniqueness and individual gifts, and also to face their unwelcome moods, their feelings of failure and guilt over unworthy behaviour. They need to learn to accept difference in themselves and others. In the Jungian psychological tradition: "To embrace weakness, liability, and darkness as part of who I am gives that part less sway over me, because all it ever wanted was to be acknowledged as a part of my whole self" (Palmer 2000, p. 71, in de Souza, 2012).

It is not appropriate to impose a sense of guilt upon children through emphasising judgement for sin. Mentioning hell can frighten little children, and incur the wrath of parents. However Christian education can add a healing dimension to dealing with the dark side of life. Through Bible stories and appropriate instruction it can introduce children to a God who loves them unconditionally, and in Jesus Christ, offers them forgiveness, and a new life of wholeness and light. The story of the Good Shepherd can help little children find a sense of safety when they are feeling "lost". For older children there are many stories about forgiveness and restoration of relationship with God: The Prodigal Son; Peter's denial that he knew Jesus; or Jacob, who cheated his brother and father, but was restored to a future life of blessing; to name a few examples. Children are often moved by an interpretation of the death and resurrection of Jesus as demonstrating his power over sin and death. The various churches have rituals of reconciliation, where children can be assured that God deals with their dark side. Even in class it is possible for children to be both affirmed in goodness, and given opportunities to address their dark side through sensitive discussion, quiet reflection and simple rituals of healing and renewal.

Conclusion

This concluding chapter has tried to address two issues which were not central in earlier chapters: the importance of formal study of the Bible and the church's teachings, and the need to acknowledge the presence of sin or darkness in the world and in human nature.

David Tacey, (2003) an Australian sociologist specialising in youth spirituality provides insights which are a fitting conclusion to this chapter and this book. He confirms that there is renewed interest in spirituality among the young which is both spontaneous and a reflection of our times. These are times when traditional religion is largely ignored or rejected, especially by the young, in favour of trusting their inner experience of spirituality. This individual spirituality is mostly inspired by their connection with nature, and expressed through the symbols and heroes of secular, electronically mediated culture. Tacey (2003) described contemporary youth spirituality as "a deeper and more profound apprehension of our ordinary lives ... a new model in which the sacred is intimate and close, a felt resonance within the self, and a deep and radiant presence in the natural world" (2003, 78-79). These observations were confirmed in the stories of many of the children in my research. This vibrant inner spirituality need not remain private but can lead to deeper connections with others, because the same spirit that is within us is within all things (2003, p. 41). However, Tacey believes that spiritual life needs to be harnessed by form or structure to be shaped and to shape the world. In stable times religion provides the individual with stability and nurture, but in times of transition, such as the present, religions such as Christianity can become rigid and authoritarian, and is rejected by many spiritually aware young people, even children, as dogmatic and irrelevant. Tacey also noted a clash between contemporary spirituality's rather naïve tendency to celebrate the good and ignore evil or sin, and what young people see as religion's preoccupation with "fall-and-redemption" theology, with its dualities of spirit and earth, spirit and body etc. (2003, p. 84).

> (Young people) should not be made to feel alienated by a formal religion that has lost its sense of the immediacy of the sacred, and that seems oblivious to the experience of transcendence that can be afforded by the natural world (Tacey, 2003, p. 82).

The challenge for the church, and for Christian religious education teachers is to bridge this gap, as it effects children, by engaging with their spirituality in all its variety, including their dark side, and providing a scaffolding of Biblically-based faith tradition on which they can grow in faith.

References

Adams, K, B. Hyde, and R. Woolley. (2008). *The Spiritual Dimension of Childhood*. Philadelphia: Jessica Kingsley.

Berryman, J. (1999). *Godly Play: A Way of Religious Education*. San Francisco: Harper.

Bingaman, K. (2001). Christianity and the shadow side of human experience. *Pastoral Psychology*, vol. 49, 3, 167-179.

Buber, M. (1970). *I and Thou*. Edinburgh: T and T Clark. Cited in Wills, R. 2012. Beyond relation: a critical exploration of 'relational consciousness' for spiritual education. *International Journal of Children's Spirituality*, vol. 17, 1, 51-60.

de Souza, M. (2012). Connectedness and *Connectedness*: the dark side of spirituality – implications for education. *International Journal of Children's Spirituality*, vol. 17, 4, 291-303.

Hay, D. (2000). Spirituality versus individualism: why we should nurture relational consciousness. *International Journal of Children's Spirituality*. vol. 5, 1. 37-48.

Hay, D. and R. Nye, (2006). *The Spirit of the Child (rev. ed.)* London: Jessica Kingsley.

Heidegger, M. (1980). *Being and Time.* Oxford: Blackwell Publishers.

Hyde, B. (2008). *Children and Spirituality: Searching for Meaning and Connectedness.* London: Jessica Kingsley.

Tacey, D. (2003). *The Spirituality Revolution – The Emergence of Contemporary Spirituality.* Sydney: HarperCollins.

Wills, R. (2012). Beyond relation: a critical exploration of 'relational consciousness' for spiritual education. *International Journal of Children's Spirituality,* vol. 17, 1, 51-60.

www.ingramcontent.com/pod-product-compliance
Lightning Source LLC
Chambersburg PA
CBHW071839230426
43671CB00012B/2000